SHATTERED TRUST:

NAVIGATING THE SHADOWS OF FRAUD IN NONPROFIT REALMS

Protect your organization's altruism and reputation from back door narcissists.

INABILITY OF LEADERS OF RELIGIOUS NOT-FOR-PROFIT ORGANIZATIONS IN NEW JERSEY TO IDENTIFY AND IMPLEMENT ADEQUATE INTERNAL ACCOUNTING CONTROLS TO DETECT AND DETER ACCOUNTING FRAUD

Wayne Balfour

MCRAESWAY
DESIGN & PUBLISHING

SHATTERED TRUST:

NAVIGATING THE SHADOWS OF FRAUD IN NONPROFIT REALMS

Protect your organization's altruism and reputation from back door narcissists.

First Printing
Shattered Trust: Navigating the Shadows of Fraud in Nonprofit Realms

ISBN: 978-1-7376627-3-0

Wayne Balfour
New Jersey, USA
vwbalfour@gmail.com

Published by:
MCRAESWAY
Tree of Life Ministries, Inc.
732.533.9090
mcraesway@gmail.com

Dedication

I dedicate this book to my Lord and Savior Jesus Christ, because he provided the grace, intelligence, and strength to complete the arduous journey. Next, I would like to dedicate this to my mother, Doreen Balfour-Moses, who always saw the best in me even though I was failing at one point during part of my high school years. Mom you were there after 24 hours of surgery to remove a tumor. Mom you were there while I was still attempting to complete homework assignments in a rehabilitation center. I will be forever grateful to you. Special thanks to my brother, Stephen, who started his doctoral journey, but never finished. He also was partly the inspiration for the pursuit of my degree. How can I forget my beautiful wife, Fior D'Aliza, who prayed and supported me in the latter part of my journey. Finally, I would like to dedicate this degree to my family and friends who supported me throughout this tumultuous expedition.

Acknowledgments

I would like to acknowledge Liberty University and staff for allowing me the blessed opportunity to complete my doctoral degree in business administration for God's glory and kingdom. The program not only refined my skills and abilities, but it certainly assisted in the development of my persistence and patience. I will be remiss not to thank God for Dr. Gene Sullivan, who patiently stuck with me despite my typos, bad grammar, and sometimes rambling paragraphs. I would also like to acknowledge Dr. Felicia Olagbemi for her well intentioned corrections that I needed to make to my paper. Apart from them, each faculty member certainly planted seeds of knowledge in my journey towards completion. I would also like to acknowledge my Pastors, Dr. and Rev. Bradley, for their continual prayers support thorough the struggles of completing my doctorate. I am grateful to my surrogate pastors Bishop and Pastor Parker.

This may come as a surprise to her, but Dr. Elaine Sanders was partly an encouragement for completing my DBA. Finally, I would like to thank Dr. Wayne Dyer and Reverend Corinthia Esaw for their kind assistance in securing interviews with their networks of religious Not for-Profit organizations.

Abstract

This study examined the inability of leaders of religious not-for-profit organizations (RNPOs) in New Jersey to identify and implement adequate accounting internal controls to detect and deter accounting fraud. Fraud affects all organizations negatively, including those that are religiously altruistic with good intentions. This study argued that protecting the organization's resources rests primarily upon the shoulders of its leaders. Previous studies argued that philanthropic organizations were more prone to fraud because of poor management, enormous trust in their employees, and poor internal accounting controls. This multi-case qualitative study studied ten RNPO leaders, validating and contradicting some previous findings of not-for-profit organizations. The conceptual framework utilized in this study was a competency-based leadership model, tone at the top or self-concept maintenance theory, the fraud triangle theory, the diamond fraud theory, and the COSO framework. The researcher used a 25-question interview guide to collect the data. The study results found larger RNPOs with larger budgets, and staff tend to have more reliable internal accounting controls, and leaders of these organizations had more specialized accounting education or experience. There were two outliers to these findings. Two organizations had larger parent organizations that oversaw all accounting functions of their local offices. The parent companies ensured that there were robust internal accounting controls. This study pointed out a few implications. Organizations need to employ a CPA or a financial professional, raise fraud awareness, and develop continuous fraud training for key leaders. Finally, RNPOs need to create and articulate their fraud policies.

Table of Contents

List of Tables

List of Figures

Section 1:

Foundation of the Study

Religious not for profit organizations (RNPOs) are intimately intertwined into every sector of society. Several major universities, hospitals, civic, and charitable organizations have religious origins. The Young Women and Men Christian Association, the Salvation Army and The Knights of Columbus are a few recognizable organizations that are RNPOs. As populations have grown worldwide and in the United States, so have social issues. The United States and other countries have seen a proliferation of RNPOs over the past century to deal with some of the social maladies that have raised its ugly head. In the United States, just about anyone can start a not for profit organization. Because of the ease of starting these organizations, fraudsters have perched and nestled in the guise of legitimate organizations. As a result, accountability and proper stewardship have become paramount for the survival and growth of legitimate organizations.

Leadership of many now defunct RNPOs found that public trust or lack thereof may have been partly to blame for the demise of their existence. Hager and Hedberg (2016) found that the news of scandals and negative press often weakened the confidence of the general public resulting in lower donations. Administrators of RNPOs have also found that the public is not just only concerned about the mission of the organization, but similarly it is also concerned about the financial stewardship of organizations. France and Tang (2018) purported that funders and donors expect not for profit (NPOs) to expound and report how they execute their activities and fulfil their commitments with donations and funding. This study examined leadership of RNPOs ability to detect and deter fraud that may potentially show its hideous head in these well intentional entities.

Background of the Problem

The problem of fraud in for-profit and not for profit entities has gone on for centuries (Zask, 2014). The devastation of accounting fraud has destroyed several companies, and thousands have lost jobs. The now infamous Enron scandal cost shareholders, pensioners, and employees $70 billion (Isa, 2011; Tak, 2015). Recine (2002) claimed that Enron's bankruptcy kindled the political reformation movement with a focus on transparency, while the WorldCom's collapse provided the momentum to push reforms through Congress. Globally according to the Association of Certified Fraud Examiners (ACFE 2020), organizations lose a median estimate of 5% of their annual revenue to various types of fraud schemes. However, less advertised fraud occurrences have happened in non or not for profit organizations (NPOs). Archambeault et al. (2015) cited in their studies that 115 incidents occurred in Non-Profit organizations from 2008 to 2011. Harris et al. (2017) acknowledged a few examples of fraud within NPOs. They included "$1.5 million of employee theft at Memorial Sloan Kettering Cancer Center, $43 million of improper payments to grantees at The Global Fund, and a $26" (p. 149). These are some statistics to attest to the depth of this problem in society. Apart from the tremendous financial losses, fraud has caused immeasurable damage to the overall economy and investor confidence (Dong et al., 2018). To restore trust in an organization's financial stability leadership of these enterprises have adopt measures such as developing a robust internal audit process, incorporating an independent board of directors and an effective audit committee to name a few (Yasin et al., 2014).

Though RNPOs are in business because of noble causes, and often the charitable or socio-economic philanthropic mission drives operations, the reality is their leadership are ultimately responsible for the proper stewardship and oversight of financial donations and stakeholders' resources. Considine et al. (2014) purported one of the challenges facing RNPOs is a lack of clarity and the lack of clear performance goals in some of these entities. Kummer et al. (2015) argued that not-for-profit organizations (NPOs) heavily depend on trust and volunteer support, as a result, some smaller NPOs may not have the relevant expertise and resources to prevent fraud.

As a result, leaders of RNPOs must heavily rely on fraud deterrent tools to act as the proverbial *basketball sixth man* to help them with the oversight of the organizations' financial resources and assets. One of the tools that management of RNPOs have used to reduce the incidence of fraud is the implementation of internal controls. Saat et al. (2013) cited Morehead (2007) that Not Profit Organizations (NPOs) who operate in a global environment have a greater propensity and are more susceptible to internal control breaches resulting in negative consequences such as fraud and corruption. Because of these issues, NPOs management through the utilization of preventive control must be diligent considering their size, location, budget, purpose, and operating environment. Saat et al. (2013) contended that NPOs should take the view that there is a direct relationship between good corporate governance and good internal control and inversely as a detective control. However, the reality the not for profit arena is equally susceptible to the ill effects of fraud, particularly with asset misappropriation, because often these entities often lack adequate controls for detecting and dealing with this issue (Archambeault et al., 2015; McDonnell & Rutherford, 2018).

Problem Statement

The general problem addressed was leaders of religious not for profit organizations and small business owners' inability to identify and implement what are adequate internal accounting controls in their organizations to deter accounting fraud (Gregory, 2017). More explicitly, the specific problem addressed was leaders of religious not-for-profit organizations' inability to identify and implement what are adequate internal accounting controls in their organizations to deter accounting fraud in the State of New Jersey. Leaders of many of these entities would love to utilize all income received to support their social or moral missions. Yallapragada et al. (2012) pointed out that according to National Fraud Center Statistics, the overall cost of white-collar crimes to the nation was $5 billion 1970, $20 billion in 1980 and $100 billion in 1990, despite the good and noble work RNPOs provide to communities. The reason for this phenomenon, according to De Armond and Zack (2017), is the perpetrators behind these deceptive acts are complex in nature. They have varying circumstances pressuring them, including different opportunities motivating them and they are justified by their different rationales. Paramount to the complexity of the perpetrators is leadership in RNPOs inability to identify and implement adequate internal controls. Archambeault and Webber (2018) and Fitzgerald et al. (2018) argued that internal controls within nonprofit organizations are especially inadequate. In response to this complex problem, the researcher proposed adopting specific leadership styles, continuous improvement of various internal controls, potential red flags for fraud, and faith-based solutions that may aid organizations in their plight.

Purpose Statement

The purpose of this qualitative case study was to explore the problem of leaders of religious not-for-profit organizations' (RNPOs) inability to identify and implement what are adequate internal accounting controls in their organizations throughout the State of New Jersey to deter various forms of accounting fraud. Religious not for profits organizations for centuries provided valuable services to their local communities worldwide. RNPOs rely heavily on grants, voluntary gifts of donors, and inexpensive or free labor of volunteers. The fundamental aim of this study was to contribute to the body of literature that exists about leaders of RNPOs understanding of governance practices of their entities, the stewardship of their entities' assets, and tools such as internal controls that are available to them thwarting would-be perpetrators of accounting fraud in their organizations (Pulido, 2018).

Nature of the Study

In general, quantitative and qualitative research methods are on two ends of the methodological continuum with mixed-method studies in the middle. Creswell and Poth (2018) and Cruz and Tantia (2017) asserted that qualitative research finds its genesis with assumptions and through the use of interpretive or theoretical framework, readers of research problems obtain the meaning of individuals or groups ascribe to a human or social problem. Because of these facts, qualitative research is one of the most popular methods used in the business and social sciences journals (Chandra & Shang, 2017; Creswell, 2014). A few more reasons for the popularity of qualitative research is it offers researchers a diverse collection of approaches, collection tools, and it primarily focuses on non-numerical data (Chandra & Shang, 2017; Thompson, 1997). The aim of qualitative research methods is to explain an experience and make meaning of experiences or phenomena (Cruz & Tantia, 2017).

Yin (2014) pointed out the aim of a multiple case qualitative method is analogous to creating an overall explanation from multiple experiments. Moreover, Creswell and Poth (2018) postulated collective or multiple case studies focused on relationship patterns opposed to a single case study, which makes it difficult to generalize because the context of cases differs.

Discussion of Method

The researcher deemed the qualitative methods was the most appropriate method for this study for a few reasons. First, the qualitative research method was embraced by the researcher because qualitative studies provided insight into broad and complex issues why leaders of RNPOs are unable to identify fraud in their organizations and the perpetrators' motives for committing crimes against institutions that serve the community (Creswell, 2016; Stake, 2010). Second, because the issue of fraud in RNPOs is both a social and business problem, the qualitative method is the most appropriate for this research study (Creswell & Poth, 2018; Cruz & Tantia, 2017). Third, because the nature of the study was primarily non-numerical and focused on relationship patterns of experience of leadership of RNPOs perspective of internal controls in the detection of fraud, the researcher believed that qualitative method was the most appropriate choice for the study.

Quantitative studies method, in contrast, is more narrowly focused on variables, their relationship, and may not explain the complexity of the perpetrators or the viewpoint of leadership of RNPOs (Creswell, 2016). Polit and Beck (2012) and Rutberg and Bouikidis (2018) contended that quantitative research method often is used to determine relationships between variables and outcomes and encompasses the development of a hypothesis or a description of the anticipated relationship, results, or expected outcomes from questions researcher attempts to answer. In the study, the researcher did not seek to develop a hypothesis, but rather, explored the human perception of leaders and their viewpoint of the impact of internal controls in detecting fraud in their organizations.

The quantitative method utilized standardized questionnaires or experiments to acquire numeric data in primarily a structured environment that afforded the researcher the ability to have control over study variables, environment, and research questions. Contrary to the use of questionnaires as done with quantitative methods, coupled with the difficulty associated with the utilization of a structured environment, this study intended to complete interviews of leaders of RNPOs in a non-controlled environment. Because of the dynamics of the quantitative method, the research deemed that it was not appropriate for this study (Polit & Beck, 2012; Rutberg & Bouikidis, 2018).

A mixed-method study essentially incorporates the best of qualitative and quantitative methods. The process of mixed research involves mixing or combining quantitative and qualitative research techniques, methods, approaches, concepts, or language into a single study (Johnson & Onwuegbuzie, 2004). The researcher desired to examine the relationship between statistical relationship between the variables of religious leaders' experiences about fraud detection and prevention in their organizations and the incorporation of internal control techniques (Creswell, 2014; Cruz & Tantia, 2017).

Discussion of Design

The researcher determined that the multiple case study qualitative design was the most appropriate because of the descriptive aspect of qualitative studies. Multi cases design tends to be more compelling and robust because of the use of multiple cases in the study (Herriott & Firestone, 1983, as cited in Yin, 2014). Ridder (2017) acknowledged one of the potential advantages of multiple case study research is the ability of researchers to complete a cross-case analysis. Yin (2014) further argued that one of the benefits of using a multi-case design, the research can validate and predict similar results or predict contrasting results. This study involved comparing the experiences of leaders of multiple RNPOs use or lack of implementation of internal controls.

Phenomenology research design, which is comprehended through single or several individual experiences, would have been challenging in this study. Phenomenological pundits aim to apprehend the meaning and common features or essences of an experience or event such as grief or anger (Creswell & Poth, 2014; Starks & Trinidad, 2007). Sokolowski (2000) identified that phenomenological statements provides researchers with information about the obvious and tells, us what we already know. The challenge with using the phenomenology research design in this study was there were variables the researcher was not aware of. Through understanding, the experiences of RNPO's leaders are necessary. The emotional experience of these administrators was inconsequential to this study.

Similarly, the grounded theory design was not chosen in this study because the grounded theory research method focuses on a process or an action that has distinct phases or steps that occur over a period (Creswell & Poth, 2018). Charmaz (2017) concluded the grounded theory design develops an interactive method from the inception of the research through the last draft of the report.

Creswell and Poth (2018) continued that researchers must recognize that there are there four specific prescribed components of the grounded theory design; causal conditions, a central phenomenon conditions, context, and consequences. However, some of the segments of the grounded theory design fit the research. The researcher did not seek to develop a theory, nor did the researcher aim to develop steps chronologically. There were challenges establishing a casual condition associated with the grounded theory design in this study.

While phenomenology design focuses on the common experiences of several individuals and grounded theory emphasizes participants' experiences in the process, the narrative design is cradled in individual stories told by participants (Creswell & Poth, 2018). The narrative design concentrates on single text data, such as transcribed interviews, to comprehend participants' experiences. Connelly and Clandinin (2006) and Clandinin et al. (2007) expounded by stating that narrative inquiry came out of a view of human experience in which humans, individually and socially, lead storied lives. People shape their daily lives by stories of who they and others are and as they interpret their past in terms of these stories. Story, in the current idiom, is a portal through which a person enters the world by which their experience of the world is interpreted and made personally meaningful. Viewed this way, narrative is the phenomenon studied in an inquiry. Connelly and Clandinin (2006) and Clandinin et al. (2007) continued the narrative inquiry deals with the study of an experience as a story. Narrative inquiry as a methodology entails a view of the phenomenon. Narrative inquiry methodology adopts a particular narrative view of experience as a phenomena under study.

The challenge with using the narrative design in this study was one matter facing RNPOs administrators was the limitation of recording and understanding of complex experiences in real-time. Fraud in most instances most likely would have occurred in the past (Keats, 2009). Another challenge with utilizing this design was researchers need to gather extensive information about the participant and have vivid understanding of the context of the individual lives at the inception of the research (Creswell & Poth, 2018). In the study of leader inability to detect fraud there are two parties involved: the leaders of RNPOs and the perpetrators. The narrative design was intended to study the experience of the leader's and perpetrator or perpetrators of the fraud. This study did not seek to understand the personal story of leaders or perpetrators, but it only sought to determine if administrators of RNPOs understanding of internal controls and its use in detecting fraud.

Finally, ethnological design typically involves the study of the procedure of learning about the way of life of a group of people with more than 20 involved in grounded theory (Creswell & Poth, 2018; Prus, 2007). Creswell and Poth (2018) stated ethnography researchers interpret and describe learned and shared patterns of values belief behaviors of culture sharing group.

Qualitative method was embraced because of its ability to examine broad complex issues, its ability to focus on relationship patterns, and its ability to examine human perceptions. In the case of this study, the qualitative method far outweighs other potential research methods. More specifically, the design of multiple case study design provided the researcher with the ability to conduct in-depth interviews with several administrators of RNPOs view of internal controls where a vivid determination was formed.

Summary of the Nature of the Study

Qualitative method was embraced because of its ability to examine broad complex issues, its ability to focus on relationship patterns, and its ability to examine human perceptions as in the case of this study far overshadows other potential research methods. More specifically, the design of multiple case study design provided the researcher with the ability to conduct in-depth interviews with several administrators of RNPOs view of internal controls where a vivid determination was formed.

Research Questions

RQ1. Is there a relationship between leadership competence, leadership style, and fraud detection?

RQ2. What mechanisms or internal controls, religious not for profits organizations have in place to prevent accounting fraud?

Conceptual Framework

The study of leaders in religious not for profit organizations (RNPOs) inability to identify and implement what are adequate internal accounting controls in their organizations to detect and deter accounting fraud is hinged upon five constructs. They are (a) competency-based leadership model, (b) At the top or self-concept maintenance theory, (c) the fraud triangle theory, (d) the diamond fraud theory, and (e) COSO framework. The first two premises speak to leadership styles and competency of accounting and management practices, the second two premises speak to why perpetrators defraud religious not for profit organizations, and the final construct discusses internal controls best practices.

Discussion of the Leadership Competency Theory

Wasylyshyn and Gronsky (2004) acknowledged that in the mid-1990s, Rohm and Haas Company, a Fortune global leader in the specialty materials industry, decided to include a more specific focus on leader behaviors in its leadership competency model. The new model at that time reflected an amalgamation of cognitive, technical, and experiential factors with key behavioral and emotional factors (i.e., emotional competence), which in the aforementioned context, emotional competence is defined as the awareness of one's own and others' feelings, and using that awareness to manage feelings as a constructive resource in achieving work objectives. Hughes et al. (2008) identified the leadership competency model as abilities, skills, knowledge, and other attributes that are relevant for a leader's success in a particular job or as identified in this study, religious leaders ability to successfully deter accounting fraud. Inherently, some religious leaders are amateurs in positions of governance in the stewardship of nonprofit organizations (NPO; Harris et al., 2017). The lack of financial and business acumen along with a lack of an understanding of internal controls leadership in RNPOs can certainly be culpable in the fraud and poor governance of their organizations. Contrarily to the aforementioned construct in the explanations of fraud in Religious Not for Profit Organizations (RNPOs), some extremely competent leaders can bypass various types of internal controls identified in the fraud theories (Harris et al., 2017). However, there are other variables that contribute to fraud in these organizations.

Tone at the Top or Self-Concept Maintenance Theory

Pundits of internal controls as a fraud deterrent have asserted that Tone at the Top or Self-concept maintenance is a critical component to proper governance in organizations. The Treadway Commission Report COSO (1987) noted that "the tone set by top management—that is the corporate environment or culture within which financial reporting occurs—is the most important factor contributing to the integrity of the financial reporting process" (Warren et al., 2015, p. 561). Warren et al. (2015) continued that the tone at top theory is broadly accepted as one of the primary predictor of ethical behavior in organizations. Pickerd et al. (2015) acknowledged based on their research of academic and practitioner literature, ethical tone at the top of an organization is a key variable in establishing successful internal control environment.

According to the COSO framework, Tone at the Top or Self Concept Maintenance is insufficient by itself. Dickins and Fay (2017) postulated though the type and number of controls an entity implements varies depending on its complexity (i.e., whether it is formation is public or non-public), the type of the industry it operates in, the geographic dispersion that it is operating (e.g., in a single country versus multi country), and the reality is strong system of internal control is extremely important to the production of reliable financial statements. Thus, leadership and management in RNPOs must understand the tone set by upper management becomes the proverbial tempo of what are the ethical expectation within the organization and continuous reinforcement of the organization's internal controls, accounting standards, and behavior.

Discussion of the Fraud Triangle Theory

Perhaps the most iconic theory used to explain why perpetrators commit fraud in organizations is Cressey's Fraud Triangle Theory (Azrina & Ling Lai, 2014; Sorunke, 2016).

Donald Cressey coined the iconic Fraud Triangle theory, which has been used to explain one of the motives for fraud for over 50 years (Jonson & Geis, 2010). Cressey (1953, as cited in Mackevicius & Giriunas, 2013) contended that the reason why people commit fraud can be cradled in three primary foundations: motivation (incentive and pressure), rationalization, and opportunity to commit fraud.

Incentive or Motivation. Mackevicius and Giriunas (2013) stated that one finding of the Fraud Triangle theory is people are motivated by selfish internal motives to commit fraud. She or he may be driven by one of three forces: (a) the presence of financial trouble, (b) a personal pressure of status aggrandizement, and (c) the pressure by employers to meet the interests of its company despite his or her own external pressure. Any of the three forces may motivate employees to bypass internal controls to satisfy the pressures (Schuchter & Levi, 2016). Houdek (2017) found that employees in various employment capacities are motivated to commit fraud for different reasons. He cited that managers are motivated by financial incentive of major bonuses based on clear performance or financial indicators set by the organization. Other employees may begin embezzling a company's resources, because of financial debts from the lack of financial means to fund their divorce, drug addiction, or student loans to name a few.

However, despite the plethora of reasons people are motived to commit fraud, Dellaportas (2013) concluded that some people are greedy and materialistic, and fraud is a means of them accomplishing their greedy desires. The motive of greed is pervasive as human motive and the world is rife with opportunity. Finally, Cressey (1953) contended that the tandem of the aforementioned factors contribute to selfish crime of fraud against organizations. This selfish crime occurs against charitable organizations because many RNPOs are selfless institutions with the sole motive of helping its community.

Rationalization. The second element of the fraud triangle construct is perpetrators psychology to rationalize and justify their reasons for committing fraud. Murphy and Free (2016) asserted that fraudsters may have an internal or external rationalization to commit fraud. Murphy and Free (2016) argued that individual's rationalization of fraud is cradled in the two theoretical foundations. Bandura (1999) and Festinger's (1957) cognitive dissonance theory claimed individuals rationalize their behavior in order to mitigate the negative emotion they experience by doing something contrary to society's or their own beliefs. Murphy and Dacin (2011, as cited in Murphy & Free, 2016) wrote about seven categories of rationalization by fraud perpetrators.

1. The seven categories of rationalizations from these two literature streams:
2. Moral justification, by reconstructing an act as being morally worthy.
3. Advantageous comparison, by comparing the act to something worse.
4. Euphemistic labeling or using convoluted language to make the act look better than is.
5. Minimize, ignore, or misconstrue the consequences of the act.
6. Denial of or blaming the victim.
7. Displacing responsibility by blaming someone else.
8. Diffusing responsibility, by blaming everyone else.

Another category labeled "entitlement" is participants' rationalization claiming they deserved extra money or organization's resources that does not belong to the perpetrator (Mayhew & Murphy, 2014; Murphy & Free, 2016). This group had an external focus; either viewing fraud from the "Robin hood" lens of moral justification where they are helping someone else with the stolen funds of from the lens where they are in denial or blaming the victim stating that "the victim deserves it" or dissemination of responsibility stating that "everyone does it" and finally displacing responsibility stating that "someone told me to do this." In either case, fraudsters found a way to justify theft of resources that did not belong to them.

Opportunity. The third factor in the Fraud Triangle theory is perpetrators perceived opportunity to commit fraud (Roden et al., 2016). Soltani (2014) acknowledged there are a number of situations in organizations that create the opportunity for white-collar criminals to commit fraud. Organizations may have ineffective monitoring of leadership by an ineffective board of directors, the dominance of some key areas of management by a single person or couple of people, high turnover in an organization, ineffective and the absence of adequate controls, and management's ability to easily override internal controls. All of the above may provide fraudsters in RNPOs the opportunity or perceived opportunity to fraudulently take the organizations assets and financial resources. Though RNPOs exist to assist humankind without the motive of profit, because of internal and external pressures, the psychological rationalization of perpetrators is that it is okay to commit fraud against the organization and the lack of internal controls in RNPOs churches, synagogues, and similar organization may have their resources stolen.

Discussion of the Fraud Diamond Theory

In later studies of why fraudsters commit crimes fraud against organizations, Wolfe and Hermanson (2004) found that in addition to incentive, opportunity, and rationalization promulgated by Cressey's fraud triangle theory, Cressey's theory may be improved by considering a fourth element-capacity. Though opportunity, incentive, and rationalization may be present, an individual personal traits and viewpoints may play a major role in whether fraud actually occurs even with the presence of the other three elements (Wolfe & Hermanson, 2004).

Capabilities. Sorunke (2016) and Schuchter and Levi (2016) contended that some individuals may not possess capability to commit fraud. These people may possess the following traits and cognitive abilities: "individual know-how," resistance to stress to ensure not being discovered immediately, confidence and ego, coercion skills to convince others concealing crimes, or use other individuals as an instrument of manipulation" (Schuchter & Levi, 2016). Some people do not desire to commit fraud because of ethical, religious, or rationalization of the risk associated with theft. This personal character trait may be more prevalent in RNPOs because some of the employees in these organizations may be motivated because of their religious beliefs (i.e., their "fear of God") or even how they may be perceived by congregants or parishioners or other members of the sect of their religious community.

COSO Framework

D'Aquila (2013) highlighted that in 1992 Committee of Sponsoring Organizations (COSO) formalized an integrated framework, perhaps representing the first major formal attempt to define internal control and provide a standard for measurement a prelude to Sarbanes-Oxley Act (SOX)—specifically, section 404 of the act—the criticality of establishing and maintaining internal controls over financial reporting. Because of the comprehensive nature of the COSO framework, the Securities Exchange Commission (SEC) and the Public Accounting Oversight Board (PCAOB) highlighted the importance of internal control as part of its regulation (D'Aquila, 2013). The SEC final rule stated, "The COSO Framework satisfies our criteria and may be used as an evaluation framework for purposes of management's annual internal control evaluation and disclosure requirement" (p. 22). D'Aquila (2013) pointed out the PCAOB embraced in its AS 2 section of its policies the COSO framework is the ideal framework when it pertains to managements' evaluation of the effectiveness of internal controls and auditors' records of financial reports. The aforementioned theories were used to establish the theoretical framework and formulate the research questions that explained the reason why fraud occurs in RNPOs, and why proper governance by leaders is critical in these organizations and why internal control strategies can help deter fraud.

Discussion of Relationship Between Research Question and Problem Statement

Leadership or management styles at the top always have or in part influenced the outcomes of organizations, especially when it related to fraud detection and prevention. Patelli and Pedrini (2015) and Schaubroeck et al. (2012) suggested that ethical leadership at the top produces a trickle-down effect and influences ethical conduct in the lower levels of organizations.

Hughes et al. (2008) identified the leadership competency model as abilities, skills, knowledge, and other attributes that are relevant for a leader's success in a particular job or as identified in this study, religious leaders ability to successfully deter accounting fraud. Faith-based or religious leaders are novices in positions of governance in the stewardship of nonprofit organizations (NPO; Harris et al., 2017). They lack the financial and business insight and understanding of internal controls. Management in RNPOs can contribute to fraud and poor governance. In contrast, some leadership styles are more apt to commit fraud because some leaders, especially those with strong accounting and financially backgrounds, may possess tremendous competence of internal accounting controls and may have the knowledge of how to bypass or override them (Dorminey et al., 2012). Therefore, an understanding for readers of the correlation of how various leadership and management styles within an organization provides an actual or perceived opportunity for malfeasants in an environment to commit fraud.

As a part of good governance, Zain et al. (2018) posited that adequate assessment of internal control is essential. AICPA (2018) defined internal control of an institution as "the plan of organization and all of the coordinate methods and measures adopted within a business to safeguard its assets, check the accuracy and reliability of its accounting data, promote operational efficiency, and encourage adherence to prescribed managerial policies." However, in Faith-Based and Religious Not for Profit organizations the existence and how well internal controls works differs from organization to organization based on various factors.

Siswantoro et al. (2018) and Kaler (2003) opined that internal controls which are necessary for the management and accountability of an organizations resources, was based on stakeholder theory which inherently promulgates that different accountability types exist. According to the stakeholder theory, accountability focuses on three stakeholders (Kaler, 2003; Siswantoro et al., 2018). The first, internally to staff and the organization's mission, second upward accountability toward donors, and finally downward accountability to the beneficiaries of an organization's outputs. Though Faith-Based and Religious Not for Profit organizations are accountable to each of the aforementioned stakeholders based on its religious teachings and mission, the reality is because of the factors identified in the Fraud Triangle theory some leaders and followers tend to commit fraud against these organization (Kaler, 2003; Siswantoro et al., 2018). One of the foremost challenges surrounding these types of organizations is financial resources and competent human capital. Often small churches do not have proper internal controls because they may not have the finances or personnel to deter risks of fraud or misappropriation effectively (Thornhill & Domino, 2016). Because of the lack of monetary resources, churches find it difficult to employee outside auditors to scrutinize their organizations' financial records (Thornhill & Domino, 2016).

Besides, not for profit organizations are more vulnerable to fraud, as they rely on trust, have weaker internal controls, and lack business and financial expertise.

Figure 1

Relationships Between Concepts

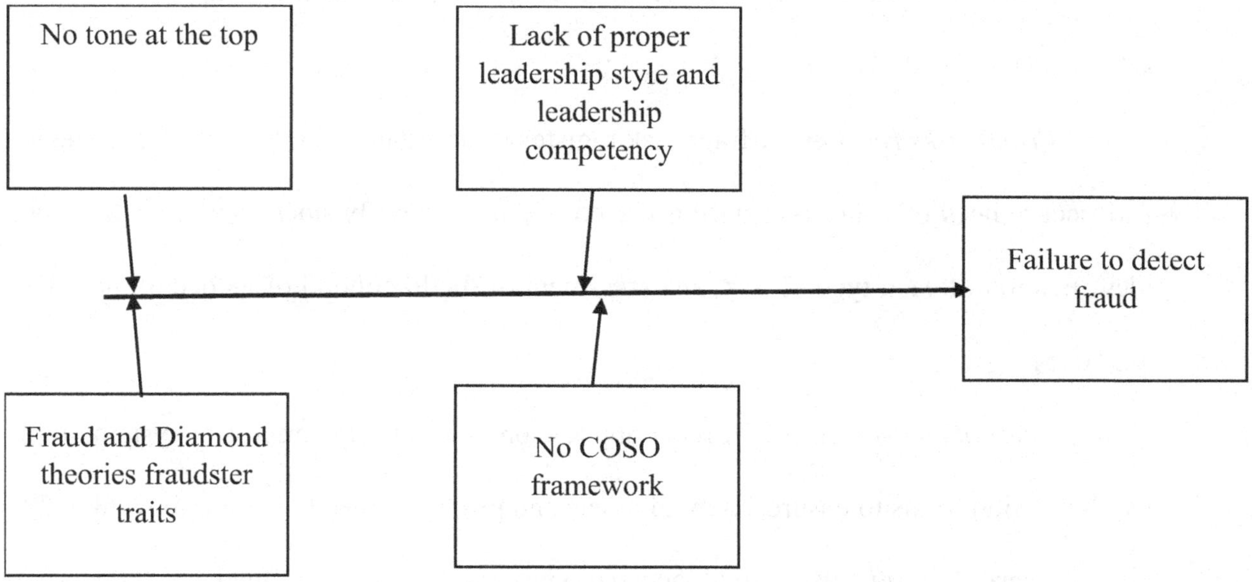

Summary of the Conceptual Framework

The study of the challenge of leaders in religious not for profit organizations' (RNPOs) inability to identify and implement what are adequate internal accounting controls in their organizations to deter accounting fraud is hinged upon five primary constructs: competency-based leadership model, at the top or self-concept maintenance theory, the fraud triangle theory, the diamond fraud theory, and COSO framework. The first two premises speak to leadership styles and competency of accounting and management practices, the second two premises speak to why perpetrators defraud religious not for profit organizations, and the final construct discusses internal controls best practices.

Definition of Terms

Control activities: "Control activities are the policies and procedures that ensure how management directives are executed. Control activities include such activities as approvals, authorizations, verifications, reconciliations, reviews of operating performance, the safeguarding of assets, and the segregation of duties." (COSO, 1992; Frazer, 2016)

Fraud risk assessment: is where an organization pinpoints the nature of the potential fraud scheme (Mock et al., 2017).

Fraud risks register: A fraud risk register is an organization's way of documenting types and occurrences of fraud risk during the course of normal business activities and includes an identification of each type of risk, an assessment of the likelihood of its occurrence (Kummer et al., 2015).

Internal controls: is the current control economic activity, process or system, implemented by all division heads to ensure safety of assets and property (Varchuk & Grabovenko, 2016).

Internal fraud: also called occupational fraud, can be defined as: "the use of one's occupation as employee, manager, or executive for personal enrichment through the deliberate misuse or misapplication of the organization's resources or assets" (Association of Certified Fraud Examiners, 2019).

Material misstatement: a significant error, either intentional or unintentional, in organizations financial statements that should have been detected or acknowledged by the organization's internal controls (Myllymäki, 2014).

Religious charity not for profit nonprofit organizations (RNPOs) or Faith based organizations (FBOs): Interchangeably terms and are churches, nonprofit employers, civic organization or any organizations that hold some type of religious underpinning or faith in their core beliefs (Yasmin et al., 2014).

Skimming: is where an employee interferes with a financial transaction, using deception and manipulation, between the business and an outside party, diverting money or assets away from the business (Kennedy, 2018).

Whistleblower: any person whether employee, vendor, former employee or anyone who possess a reasonable belief that the information they are providing relates to a possible securities law violation, fraud or misrepresentation of information that violates Sarbanes Oxley Act (Chen, 2018; 17 C.F.R. § 240.21F-2(b)(1), 2013).

Assumptions, Limitations, Delimitations

To assist readers with the scope of this study the research discussed the assumptions, limitations, and delimitations in the next section.

Assumptions

With all academic work, assumptions act as the underpinning and can be seen as something researchers hold as true without tangible proof (Ellis & Levy, 2009). Creswell and Poth (2018) posited that qualitative research such as this study begins with assumptions and informs readers of the problem studied and provides meaning to the individuals or groups.

This study pivoted on two premises. The first assumption of this study was administrators or leaders of RNPOs were honest and truthful during the interviews about their understanding of what is fraud, fraud prevention, fraud detection techniques, and internal controls. Dresser (2013) found when interviewees personal interests conflicted with the strains of participation, some subjects covertly broke the rules of engagement. Though religious leaders of RNPOs or faith-based organizations (FBOs) were expected to be honest about their understanding of the terms as mentioned earlier, the reality was the perception of leaders' ignorance, and the anxiety of an interview could cause the subjects to misrepresent their knowledge of the terms mentioned earlier in their organization. To mitigate this risk, I provided the interviewees with definitions of the terms before the interviews to reduce ambiguity.

The second assumption couched in this qualitative study was the researcher understands the research must be scrubbed from personal beliefs and values. Muganga (2015) found that in qualitative research, researchers can impact the outcome of data interpretation with their personal bias and prejudices. To mitigate this challenge, reflexivity was incorporated (Lee et al., 2015). Lee et al. (2015) argued that if a researcher filters the research through a reflection of the entire research context and process, the researcher is systematically attending to determine their effect on the study, and how these values actions, attitudes, and beliefs impact knowledge construction.

Limitations

Like assumptions, qualitative limitations are external conditions and internal weaknesses that threaten the dependability, transferability, conformability, and credibility of the research design and may affect the outcome of the research (Bloomberg & Volpe, 2012). The primary limitation of this study was the researcher intended to have a purposeful sample of interviewees for the study, but the reality was the author was limited to the willingness of leadership in RNPOs to participate in the interviews. The second and equally salient limitation was the qualitative multi-case study was restricted to RNPOs located in the state of New Jersey. A final limitation was not all RNPOs may follow General Accepted Accounting Principles (GAAP) or Financial Accounting Standards Board (FASB) internal accounting documents, practices, or operational processes. An organization may have adopted unorthodox accounting practices.

Delimitations

Delimitation is a term used in qualitative research and helps readers understand the situation and whether findings from the case apply to their settings (Alpi & Evans, 2019). It is also the exclusionary and inclusionary boundaries set by researchers of objectives, research questions, variables, theoretical objectives, and targeted population (Simon & Goes, 2013). As a result, the researcher reduced the geographical scope of the study to Religious Not for Profit and Faith-Based organizations in the State of New Jersey. Other states or United States territories were not included. In addition, the researcher conducted qualitative research of church administrators, pastors, Rabbis, Iman's, financial administrators, the board of trustees of religious groups to saturation point, who was willing to have an interview with the researcher. Also, the study only looked at internal fraud committed by leadership or people associated with the organizations. External stakeholder and external fraud were not part of the study. The study only looked at two leadership or stewardship styles-Tone at Top and leadership competency theory. Other leadership styles that may contribute to fraud were not part of the study. The study also included fraud detection techniques used by RNPOs in the state of New Jersey to include whistleblower policies, GAAP and accounting training to employees, fraud registry, management information system mechanisms, and internal control review. On the other hand, the study does not include fraud committed by external stakeholders, fraud committed in other states and territories outside of New Jersey, and fraud committed in for-profit organizations.

Significance of the Study

Not for profits have played an essential role in the economy and society throughout the world for centuries. United States' residents contribute over half a trillion dollars annually in donations and volunteering of time (Winterich & Zhang, 2014). Haynes (2009) posited that Faith-Based Organizations societally deliver a variety of services to the public in the form of elderly care, justice advocacy for the oppressed and humanitarian aid, and international development efforts. Lunn (2009) opined that Religious Not for Profit organizations are perceived as being more trustworthy than governments, and more sensitive to the local needs. Trust or actual level of assurance of the nonprofit sector has spurred the public to become better candidates for supporting nonprofit organizations through charitable giving (Hager & Hedberg, 2016). However, the lack of trust and assurance could be detrimental or perhaps fatal not only to the organization, but the perception of the motive of the entire not for profit sector. Lee et al. (2017) found when social ventures have a for-profit alignment, the perception of the public is the project is greed-driven, and consumer perceptions and support are opposed to it.

Conversely, with not for profit organizations, the perception of people is favorable because the cause is designed to be communal and in the interest of the society. The public confidence in the effectiveness and pro-social alignment of the nonprofit sector, especially with community organizations, translates into a belief in their effectiveness and worth, thereby prompting our monetary gifts (Hager & Hedberg, 2016). Religious not for profits are intimately interwoven into society. This study would add to the potential societal effect of and erosion of the public trust when leaders of these organizations fail to address the importance of internal controls to detect and prevent fraud in their organizations. Though leaders of religious not for profit organizations should focus on the social mission, paramount in its goal and stewardship is providing transparency and confidence to its constituents by ensuring proper and effective internal controls.

Reduction of Gaps

Fraud in for-profit organizations have made national and international media headlines. Salin et al. (2017) pointed out that it is difficult to escape from the corporate financial fraud highlighted by the media. While there is extensive research examining financial statement fraud, there is little research exploring asset diversions in the nonprofit sector (Harris et al., 2017). This research not only expounds on fraud in the not for profit sector, but it includes fraud and fraud detection in religious not for profit and faith-based organizations, specifically in the state of New Jersey.

Implications for Biblical Integration

Twentieth first-century businesses and organizations can find many of their fundamental tenets in the Bible, especially when it comes to the proper governance and stewardship of resources to detect and deter fraud. Though the scriptures do not explicitly speak about fraud against religious not for profit organizations, it does discuss proper relationships that can be applied to any organization. Van Duzer (2010) pointed out that human beings in the Genesis account of creation are called to provide governance of God's creation and resources. Genesis 1: 28 states, "God blessed them and said to them, fill the earth and take control of it. Rule over the fish in the sea and the birds in the air. Rule over every living thing that moves on the earth" (Easy Reading Version). Stewardship began in the Garden of Eden in the Genesis account and continues throughout each century in the Bible, according to scriptures. Some of the notable accounts of stewardship can be seen in the life of Noah leading his family through the flood Genesis 7-8 KJV; Moses leading his people out of Egypt Exodus 4-15; David leading his people through several wars and civil unrest; 1 Samuel 18-30 KJV to the Apostles leadership of the church in the New Testament. Paul, the

Apostle, in his letter to Timothy, highlights one of the critical qualifications of leadership in 1 Timothy 3:8, it is that they are not greedy of gain (King James Version). God has always required someone to govern his people and resources honestly and successfully. Shaharuddin and Sulaiman (2015) acknowledged that management is accountable to its stakeholders; the greatest of them God.

The Garden of Eden was a utopian experience marked by a perfect relationship between man and God. However, after the sinful fall of Adam, the ideal relationship with God and humanity and humankind with others unraveled which climax marked by the banishment of humanity from the garden. Genesis 3 (King James Version). A slow and downward spiral of human interaction with God and social interaction with themselves continued. Paul, the Apostle, coined humankind problem in Roman 5:16, "in a nutshell: one person did it wrong and got us in all this trouble with sin and death" (The Message Version). God, in His divine wisdom, saw the necessity of the Ten Commandments and other civil commandments to assist how man was to interact with God and how humans should interact with humans. The first five of Ten Commandments outline how humans should relate to God, and the second five outlines how humans should live with each other (Fredriksen, 2014). One commandment that God admonishes humans to obey is one should not covet another man's property. One of the contributing factors to fraud in organizations is individuals unlawfully wanting the organization's resources. The Old Testament Ecclesiastics 5:10 warns "he that loveth silver shall not be satisfied with silver, nor he that loveth abundance with increase: this is also vanity" (King James Version). The New Testament scriptures continue in 1 Timothy 6:10, "For the love of money is the root of all evil: which while some coveted after, they have erred from the faith, and pierced themselves through with many sorrows" (King James

Version). The love of money has caused people throughout scriptures to make poor decisions as it pertains to their lives. Poor decision making has not only negatively influenced the person, but it has also negatively affected associated organizations.

The scriptures explicitly state in 1 Thessalonians 4:16 that no man transgress and overreach his brother and defraud him in this matter or defraud his brother in business. For the Lord is an avenger in all these things, as we have already warned you solemnly and plainly told you. Greed is not the only reason why people commit fraud. As previously indicated, Cressey's (1953) Fraud Triangle identifies rationalization opportunity and pressure are variables that cause fraudsters to commit these egregious crimes against their organizations.

To assist humans in overcoming this type of behavior, the Bible through God's Word provides a solution beyond the Ten Commandments through his Son Jesus Christ. Romans 8:3, "God has done what was impossible for the Law since it was weak because of selfishness. God condemned sin in the body by sending his own Son to deal with sin in the same body as humans, who are controlled by sin" (Common English Bible). God continues in Romans 12:2 admonishes readers, "not conformed to this world: but be ye transformed by the renewing of your mind, that ye may prove what is that good, and acceptable, and perfect, will of God" (King James Version). Having a new perspective of God's will include employees of RNPOs not defrauding their organizations.

In conclusion, although the temptation to commit fraud against not for profit organizations exists, through the knowledge of the scriptures and love for God individuals can overcome the temptation. Religious not for profit organizations can serve their communities and do the work of God without any impediments with all the donated resources that donors gave them.

Relationship to Field of Study

As previously indicated, charitable giving in the United States to religious not for profit and faith-based organizations have reached an all-time high of $410 billion (Giving USA, 2017). Because of the complexity of operating RNPOs, the pressure of donors and funders, and the possible catastrophic effects of fraud in RNPOS, proper accounting, governance, and transparency is now a paramount necessity in these organizations (Arvidson & Lyon, 2014). In addition, religious not for profits have become partners with the government in building communities. Government takes an intrinsic role in the community work, supported by nonprofit organizations (Arvidson & Lyon, 2014). As a result, it imperative that religious not for profit organizations strengthen all weakness, which includes preparing accurate financial statements for internal and external stakeholders. Proper accounting has become a mechanism for RNPOs in its effort to combat fraud and provide transparency to stakeholders. To thwart accounting fraud, the GASB Statement of Financial Accounting Standards No. 117, Financial Statements of Not for Profit Organizations acts as the cornerstone of nonprofit financial reporting (Elson et al., 2007; Enofe & Amaria, 2011).

Summary of the Significance of the Study

In conclusion, RNPOs are implanted into the fabric of society, and their existence has benefited billions of people around the globe. Financial schemes against these entities is a major communal problem because the devastating implications are generally financial, economical, sociological, emotional, and psychological, potentially causing the public to reduce or stop supporting these vital organizations that partner with government and communities across the world. This qualitative multi-case study adds to the body of knowledge that can assist RNPO administrators in reducing the gaps and halt the potential issues associated with the malady of fraud in RNPOs. The next section of the paper reviewed and expounded on related research and literature that relates to the problem fraud and leadership inability to detect and prevent fraud in RNPOs.

A Review of Professional and Academic Literature Review

Amiram et al. (2018) acknowledged COSO/ACFE's Fraud Risk Management Guide (2016) definition of fraud as any intentional act or deletion of data designed to deceive others, resulting in the victims experiencing a loss and/or the perpetrator achieving a gain. Omidi et al. (2019) offered the occurrence of fraud is when malfeasants-in-disguise intentionally manipulated the books or misstate financial records. Unfortunately, the sensationalization of the repercussions of fraud are well-documented in the media, and multiple studies have been done about for-profit organizations and corporations. Sorunke (2016) pointed out that fraud in the corporate sector has been comprehensively studied, resulting in a well-established theoretical framework.

Inversely, fraud in religious not for profit organizations (RNPOs) has had little attention. The reality is the cost and damage associated with fraud in RNPOs cannot fully be calculated because the trust of donors and other implications associated with fraud is not easily calculated. Hou et al. (2017) opined that trust is the dynamic that motivates both prospective and actual donors, and broken or damaged trust is an obstacle that prevents the public from giving donations due to adverse events such as fraud. Brown (2001) found the dynamic of trust is one of the most significant challenges facing RNPOs or FBOs apart from its mission of how to go about implementing their mission. RNPOs or FBOs greatest challenge is understanding their fiscal responsibilities to the millions of individual donors and agencies that support them through continuing funding for the specific purpose of them fulfilling those missions and goals (Brown,

2001). The literature review presented in this study builds a conceptual framework, a scholarly overview of the significant contemporary constructs, shows issues related to fraud and leadership ability, and recognizes and deters fraud in RNPOs (Lenz et al., 2017).

Overview of Not for Profit Organization

Religious not for profit organizations (RNPOs) or faith-based organizations (FBOs) as they are sometimes termed, are organizations that are created with noble missions, causes, and goals. Backer (2016) noted that religion plays an unquestionable and essential role in encouraging many citizens to achieve social consciousness and action. Backer (2016) opined that about two-thirds of Americans embrace the belief that houses of worship contribute to solving critical social problems. Yasmin et al. (2014) pointed out that the term "faith-based and religious charity organizations are often used interchangeably and are involved in activities that often shaped by their faith" (p. 104). Clarke and Ware (2015) found that religious non-government organizations (RNGOs) in Australia, which are similar to religious not for profits or nonprofit organizations (RNPOs) in the United States, are branded by their missions rooted in religious and spiritual beliefs. Clarke and Ware (2015) argued that an intersection could be found between FBOs and RNGOs because both are driven by their religious teachings of all faiths, including not just Christian, but also Buddhist, Hindu, Jewish, and Muslim organizations.

Gamble and Beer (2017) and DiMaggio and Anheier (1990) purported that historically not for profits (NFPs) are formally recognized Internal Revenue Service (IRS) organizations that are financial outlets for benevolence and altruistic behavior. Often, these institutions are associated with religious institutions or ideologies and tend to view the success of their organizations based on whether or not it is fulfilling its organization mission, which is usually a spiritual and social agenda, but can pursue for profit social ventures to address social issues and have the ability to retain profit.

RNPOs or FBOs are not alike with how they incorporate their religious viewpoints in the delivery of social and educational services. The religious views of these organization range from its religious philosophy totally immersed to lightly sprinkles in the delivery of services. Nevertheless, FBO organizations are classified as (a) faith-permeated organizations, (b) faith-centered organizations, (c) faith-affiliated organizations, and (d) faith-background organizations (Crofts, 2014; Sider & Unruh, 2004).

Faith-permeated organizations are marked by their religious faith permeating across all levels of the organization and have clear terms of governance, mission, staffing, and support (Crofts, 2014; Sider & Unruh, 2004). The delivery of these organizations' social service programs are threaded with explicit religious content (Crofts, 2014; Sider & Unruh, 2004). These RNPOs believe the religious dimension is necessary to their social service delivery. As a result, individual workers are often required to participate in religious worship and may also be required to sign or agree to a faith declaration explicitly.

Faith-centered organizations were founded primarily for religious purposes and remained strongly connected to the religious community through funding sources and affiliation and require the governing board and most staff to share the organization's faith commitments (Crofts, 2014; Sider & Unruh, 2004). Social service delivery incorporates overtly religious messages, but clients have the option not to participate in these activities and still receive benefits of the program (Crofts, 2014; Sider & Unruh, 2004). Faith-affiliated organizations have links with and are influenced by their religious founders, but do not require staff to participate in religious activities or affirm their religious faith (Crofts, 2014; Sider & Unruh, 2004). Service delivery incorporates little or no explicitly religious content, although spiritual resources may be made available to clients.

Lastly, faith-background organizations tend to look and act like secular organizations, although they do have a historical tie to a faith tradition (Crofts, 2014; Sider & Unruh, 2004). Faith commitments are not considered in the selection of staff and board, and these organizations do not expect participants or the organizations' religious experience to contribute to program outcomes. An example of this is community development corporations (CDCs). Lowe and Shipp (2014) found that black church CDCs facilitated partnerships in their communities that aided in building capacity by aggregating technical assistance, financial support, and human capabilities to meet community needs without any religious strings attached to participants.

RNPOs are multi-faceted and complex organizations. On one end of the faith continuum, RNPOs are faith-infused entities requiring both participants and staff to sign or agree to a faith declaration explicitly. On the other end of the spectrum, RNPOs have a faith-centered background but do not require their staff or participants to commit to any religious activity. Faith background organizations only point to their origins, but the faith indoctrination in their delivery of service is not required. The religious diversity of RNPOs shows how complex and diverse they can be. It is imperative for administrators to incorporate robust internal controls to nullify the complications of the staffing and volunteer composition of RNPOs.

Diversity of Religious Not for Profit Organizations

There were an estimated 350,000 religious congregations in the United States, and 314,000 were considered Christian faith in nature (Roland & Harris, 2014). Van Gelder and Zscheile (2018) acknowledged that as of 2010, there were almost 60 million Catholics and virtually the same number of Protestants in the United States. Zurlo (2015) opined that Christianity was instrumental in the development of the field of sociology in the early twentieth century. The Christian social gospel movement that peaked in the 1920s primarily focused on the idea that Christians were obligated and responsible to urbanize and industrialize the world with the application of Judeo Christian values and ethics to societal problems for the coming kingdom of God (Zurlo, 2015). Whether protestant or catholic, one of the common threads of the social outreach movement was taking the philosophical teachings of Jesus to go into the entire world and help churches adopt the philosophical viewpoint of helping humankind. Almost all hospitals in the United States found their origins from Christian churches, in particular the Catholic Church (Corporate Works, 2014). Similarly, the Protestant churches were equally instrumental in founding colleges.

As one can expect, Christianity is immersed in houses of worship, hospitals, and colleges, but one may be surprised that Christianity also sprinkled in the origins of more notable organizations such as the Boy Scouts of America, Girl Scouts of America, Young Women Christian Association (YMCA), and Young Men Christian Association (YMCA). However, because of the religious diversity of immigrants who have moved to the United States, religious organizations are not only Christian, but also include Muslims, Buddhists, Hindus, Sikhs, Jewish, and others. Several Jewish infused organizations are involved in philanthropic works. For instance, Nasatir and Friedman (2014) acknowledged that through the Jewish United Fund (JUF), the Jewish Federation of Metropolitan Chicago in March 2008 launched the JUF Right Start Jewish Early Childhood Initiative. The program provided vouchers of up to $2,000 to young families who had never had a child enrolled in a Jewish preschool, as an incentive to send children to five-day-a-week program in a Jewish preschool of their choice. This is an example of initiatives of Jewish RNPOs that are not well publicized to the public.

Nonetheless, between 1970 and 2010, Protestant churches like the Southern Baptist and Assemblies of God have seen a modest total net increase (Van Gelder & Zscheile, 2018). In contrast, over the same period, the Catholic Church has seen a decline in their congregations. The decrease in Catholicism and the modest increase in Protestant church attendance may be explained by the rise in population, a shift in the family make up from two-parent to one-parent families, immigration patterns, and technology to name a few (Van Gelder & Zscheile, 2018).

The entry of immigrants since the passing of the Hart-Celler Act of 1965 has given rise to greater racial and ethnic diversity in the United States, especially in the Latino and Asian communities (Pyong & Sou, 2015). These two-immigrant groups' post-1965 eras accounted for over 75% of total immigrants. While Latino immigrants are predominantly Christian, Asian immigrant groups are primarily non-Christian, while many Asian immigrants are Muslims, Buddhists, Hindus, and Sikhs contributing to religious pluralism in the United States (Pyong & Sou, 2015). Pyong and Sou (2015) found that over 80% of co-ethnic Asian Hindu, Buddhist, and Sikh groups in their study participated in a religious institution. In addition, there were high levels of participation of Asian Christian groups, namely Korean and Vietnamese Catholic groups, in a co-ethnic church.

The immigrant diversity of RNPOs and FBOs in the United States produces challenges to administrators of these organizations. The primary challenge for leaders of these organizations is a dichotomy viewpoint where perpetrators' philosophical perspective may be it is natural to commit fraud in the immigrants' country of origin. For example, Isaksson (2015) pointed out that Sub-Saharan Africa based houses are some of the world's most corrupt and ethnically-fragmented countries and corruption varies systematically depending on the ethnic group affiliation within each country. Therefore, having a diligent system to detect and stop fraud is paramount to the mission of organizations.

RNPOs Sources of Revenue

FBOs and RNPOs survival and existence are heavily dependent upon grants and donations of various stakeholders. In 2017, Americans for the first time in history gave over $400 billion to religious organizations, education, human services, foundation health organizations, art, culture, humanities, and international affairs (Giving USA, 2018). Of the over $400 billion that the public gave out in 2017, $127 billion or over 30% of all donations went to religious organizations (Giving USA, 2018). Of the over $400 billion donated, individuals accounted for 70% of all donations. Corporations, foundations, and endowments gave the remaining 30% of donations (Giving USA, 2018). Because of this, it is critical for RNPOs to strengthen their relationship with stakeholders, especially with individuals because as Ramanath (2016) noted, annually at least half of all first-time donors to a Non-Governmental Organizations (NGO) or RNPO do not donate a second time; and among repeat donors, it is not uncommon that the loss rates are as high as 30% annually.

In sum, first impressions are lasting impressions to donors. As a result of the scarce resources available to RNPOs, management of these organizations must provide potential donors, current donors, and stakeholders, assurances the resources it gives to these entities includes strong leadership and diligent internal controls not only in current business practices, but for their future survival and growth. As previously stated, administrators of RNPOs have found that the public is not only concerned about the mission of the organization, but the public is usually worried about the financial stewardship of their organizations.

Overview of Fraud

The frequency or more particularly the infrequency of giving by donors makes vigilance governance and stewardship of RNPOs funds significant for their survival and growth. The exposure of fraud in organizations can have damaging reactions and an adverse effect on an entities credibility, especially with the advent of powerful online communication tools like social media and blogs. Negative comments can bring harmful results and long-lasting consequences that could cripple or put organizations out of business (Milde & Yawson, 2017).

To determine the risk associated with fraud, it is imperative for leaders of RNPOs to understand what fraud is. Jackson (2015) identified financial fraud as the act of deception and misrepresentation with the intent to deceive. Both financial fraud and financial exploitation share the similarly of perpetrators using a position of trust to exploit a person or an organization's assets (Jackson, 2015). More formally, the Association of Certified Fraud Examiners (ACFE, 2019a) defined internal fraud, also known as *occupational fraud*, as: "the use of one's occupation for personal enrichment through the deliberate misuse or misapplication of the organization's resources or assets." Or simply stated, this type of fraud occurs when "an employee, manager, or executive commits fraud against his or her employer" (Sabau, 2012, p. 111).

According to Gibson (2017), non-occupational fraud occurs when a vendor, customer, or client defrauds an organization of its resources. An example of non-occupational fraud is when a vendor has insider trading information about a company that she or he can sell to gain a financial advantage. ACFE (2019a) developed the most comprehensive taxonomy fraud classification model. Better known as the 'fraud tree,' the model outlines 49 different individual fraud schemes, grouped into three main categories and a few subcategories.

ACFE summarizes the 49 types into three broad categories, which are:

1. Assets misappropriation;
2. fraudulent statements; and
3. corruption.
4.

Table 1

ACFE Fraud Classification

Asset Misappropriation	Financial Statement	Corruption
Skimming of cash	Asset and revenue overstatement	Illegal gratuities
Theft of inventory	Asset and revenue understatement	Bribery
Theft of office equipment		Conflict of interest
		Economic extortion
Fraudulent disbursements		Financial kickbacks

Adapted from "ACFE Fraud Tree."

Asset misappropriation is the most common type of fraud carried out by schemers and is concocted primarily by lower-level employees (O'Gara, 2014). Members of management are also malefactors of this type of fraud; the primary difference is the size of the organizations' loss. According to ACFE's (2020) report to the nations, management misappropriated an average of $850,000 or six times what other lower level employees stole from organizations. O'Gara (2014) suggested that not only employees and management misappropriate organizations' resources, but customers, vendors, and other third parties may act as fraudsters. The primary methods of asset misappropriation fraud include theft by employees in the form of cash and assets, embezzlement, payment scams, and fraudulent disbursement (ACFE, 2019b; Tinkelman & Song, 2012). Not-for-profits face the risk of fraud in many areas, including risk associated with donations. Murphy

(2015) identified the following are some common misappropriation of funds fraud issues that not-for-profits may encounter.

1. Abuse of credit card privileges for personal use.
2. Forgery of checks by using RNPOs checks for personal bills and individual purchases.
3. Stolen donations, especially with significant cash transactions events with little or no oversight.
4. Forgery of checks.
5. Misclassification of restricted donations.

A study conducted by the association of certified fraud examiners found that in 114 countries, 83% of all fraud was the misappropriation of funds. This type of fraud is not reported by 66% of corporations, and as much as 95% of all fraud in churches goes undetected (ACFE, 2020; Majid et al., 2016; Palvo, 2013; Thornhill & Domino, 2016). Clearly, the misappropriation of funds is an epidemic in many types of organizations throughout the world.

Financial statement fraud conversely is more likely to occur in RNPOs and other nonreligious organizations by highly skilled employees who understand accounting practices. Albrecht et al. (2015) cited that financial statement fraud is ordinarily a top-down type of fraud that adversely influences individuals, organizations, and society. This type of fraud almost always involves collusion of an organization's employees, but is not limited to a combination of lower-level employees and almost always includes one or more of executive management such as the chief executive officer (CEO), chief financial officer (CFO), and chief operations officer (COO), manipulating the financial statements because of some type of internal or external pressure to show an excellent performance of the organization (Albrecht et al., 2015). As previously stated, it involves overstatement or understatement of the financial position of the entity. The Association of Certified Fraud Examiners' Report to the Nations on Occupational Fraud and Abuse reported that financial statement fraud accounts for nine percent of all fraud, amounting to nearly $1 million per occurrence and accounts for billions lost by organizations annually (ACFE, 2019a).

The final general area of fraud RNPOs are most likely to incur is corruption. According to ACFE (2019a), corruption can be defined as the wrongful use or influence for another person or the employee or in the case of RNPO administrators, and/or volunteers contrary to their duties or rights as principal or agent of that organization. There are two types of bribery associated with corruption (ACFE, 2019a). The first is commercial bribery, where a private individual engages in a commercial transaction with the intent to obtain a commercial or business competitive advantage. The second is official bribery, where a government official uses his or her position to unduly influence an act of government. Some methods of corrupt payment include the following: (a) inappropriate or excessive gifts, (b) loans which in some case that will never be repaid, (c) the use of the organizations credits cards to make personal payments to the fraudster, (d) sexual favors in lieu of the organization's assets, (e) overpayment of purchase with the intent to receive kickbacks, (f) free use of the organization's property for rent or the use of the organization's vehicles for free and not for organization's business hidden ownership interest, (g) selling or leasing the organization's assets for less than fair market value with the intent of obtain *quid pro quo* or kickbacks, or (h) simply promise of favorable treatment (ACFE, 2019a). This is a comprehensive list of possible corruption that may occur in RNPOs that may be ignorantly or deliberately done.

RNPOs or FBOs are more susceptible to each type of fraud mentioned. Depending on the size of the organization, these types of crimes can go undetected for years. Churches primarily take cash offerings and if there are no checks and balances, a fraudster can skim cash undetected without anyone's knowledge. In the case of financial statement fraud, many RNPOs afford key players an incredible amount of trust, and the manipulation of statements can be easily done. RNPOs or FBOs are at higher risk for corruption. Without internal controls, a small loan may never be paid back and may go undetected for years without administrators being aware. The use of the organization's vehicle for non-business related activities by the volunteers or an entities staff may be part of the culture. Volunteers may see it as reimbursement for their services, although they are volunteers. Sex for the use of the entities' assets certainly is complicated to trace in an audit. All the above are crimes against RNPOs and reflect a tiny number of possible scenarios that may undermine many of these organizations' ability to effectively deliver their services to the communities they serve. Administrators and management may have tremendous leadership skills in developing the organizations, but may lack the financial competence of how to implement proper internal controls.

Atmosphere for Fraud

Fraud does not always happen in a silo. Multiple factors contribute to fraud, ranging from fraudsters psychological traits to inadequate internal controls. Fraud is the deliberate act by one or multiple individuals to deceive or mislead the entity's stakeholders to misappropriate assets of an organization, distorting an organization's financial performance, or otherwise obtaining an unfair advantage (Hemraj, 2004). Fraud involves the use of deception to secure an unjust or illegal financial advantage, and incorporates white-collar crime, defalcation, irregularities, and embezzlement misappropriation of a company's assets or the manipulation of its financial data to the advantage of the fraudster (Hemraj, 2004). However, the reality of financial accounting involved may include financial errors or misstatements (Lenghel, 2015). Acknowledged errors can refer either to the prior fiscal year or to the current fiscal years (Lenghel, 2015). These errors include the effects of mathematical mistakes, errors in the application of accounting policies, ignorance, or wrong interpretation of events. The atmosphere for fraud may capitalize on a perceived or actual mistake in financial accounting statements. However, Cressey Fraud Triangle may provide some of the ingredients for the perfect atmosphere for fraud outside of errors that schemers may take advantage in financial statements.

Overview of the Fraud Triangle

There is no contemporary discussion about fraud without a discussion of Dr. Donald Cressey's classic work of the Fraud Triangle. Akers and Matsueda (1989) opined that Cressey made some of the most fundamental contributions to the field of social psychology of crime. Jacobs (1954) highlighted in his book review of Cressey's provocative writing about white-collar crime that Cressey abandoned legal concepts of fraudsters and developed two criteria for classifying a malfeasant as an embezzler. Jacobs (1954) pointed out that Cressey's study argued that fraudsters must have a putative position of trust in good faith and the person must have violated the trust by committing a crime. Jacob (1954) expounded that Cressey identified three common variants are always present in the psyche or mind-set of fraudsters that commit fraud. First, rationalization is referred to by Cressey to mean malfeasants state of mind, which enables them to violate the trust, and at the same time, look upon herself or himself as a non-violator and in no sense a criminal. Second, there must be an opportunity to commit the crime. Finally, the perpetrator must have internal or external pressure or motivation to commit the fraudulent act.

Opportunity.

Figure 2

Fraud Triangle

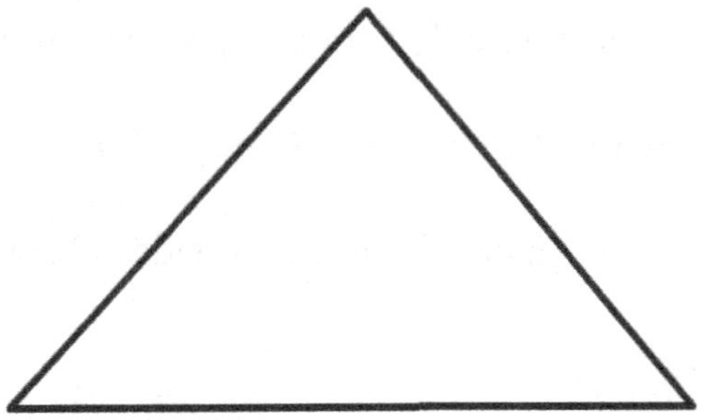

Rationalization Motivation

Rationalization. Rationalization or criminal justification is a mental process that aligns a person's morally dubious behavior with their values or ethical standards in such a way that the person perceives themselves as moral, despite their immoral behavior (Houdek, 2017; Shalv et al., 2015). Fraudsters somehow find a way to justify the theft of resources that did not belong to them. Houdek (2017) continued that if an employer negatively changes employees' benefits, such as increasing the cost of health care, employees in their own eyes may interpret it as an injustice done to them. Their immoral behavior is justified, and they do not consider themselves as dishonest. For example, a volunteer or employee of a RNPOs may believe that using the entity's vehicle for personal use may justify the lack of competitive pay they receive or the use of the entities' telephone for long-distance calls without paying for the volunteer hours they serve in the food pantry. In each example, volunteers and employees of RNPOs commit an immoral act, but believe the behavior is justifiable.

Opportunity. The second condition that exists in Cressey's Fraud Triangle is perpetrators' perceived or actual opportunity to commit fraud. There are many situations in organizations that create the opportunity for white-collar criminals to commit fraud (Roden et al., 2016; Soltani,

2014). Roden et al. (2016) embraced the Statement of Auditing Standards AU-C 240 as the framework and context of their research of all three sides of the fraud triangle (opportunity, pressure, and rationalization). Organizations may have one or a combination of weaknesses that exist that malfeasants may exploit (Roden et al., 2016). The following are a few of the weaknesses that may exist in an organization that culprits of fraud may take advantage of (a) ineffective monitoring by an inept board of directors, (b) the dominance of some critical areas of management by a single person or couple of people, (c) high turnover in an organization, (d) ineffective and the absence of adequate internal controls, and (e) management's ability to easily override internal controls. All of the above may provide fraudsters in RNPOs the opportunity or perceived opportunity to siphon off the organizations' assets and financial resources fraudulently.

Incentive or Motivation. Cressey's research of white-collar criminals pointed out the third condition that exists among all interviewees was pressure or motive. Huang et al. (2017) submitted that motivation to commit fraud results from the perceived or actual weight on a person for various reasons. Nindito (2018) acknowledged that incentive, pressure, or motivation is a variant that inspires a person to commit fraud and may include features such as lifestyle, economic demands, as well as the perpetrators' environment. Nindito (2018) contended that there are four types of pressure that fraudsters face: (a) personal financial needs, (b) financial instability, (c) internal organizational pressure, and (d) external environmental pressures. In some cases, the motive to commit fraud, especially from a managerial level, may be external when financial stability or profitability is threatened by industry, economic, or an entity's operating conditions (Huang et al., 2017). Schuchter and Levi (2016) posited that one of the incentives for perpetrators of fraud is financial greed. Some people live beyond their means, and the motive to steal from their employer is heightened. In addition, greed and personal aggrandizement and sociopathic behavior may motivate fraudsters in an organization. All or one of the aforementioned motives may exist in RNPOs. Although it may be a not for profit organization, the reality is the same psychological pressure can tempt employees to decide to defraud the organization. One of the challenges leadership in RNPOs are faced with is people are incredibly complex. Thus, having robust internal controls in place may be necessary to thwart would-be fraudsters.

Fraud Diamond Theory

Although Cressey Fraud Triangle theory (FTT) has been embraced by many auditors and fraud examiners as the gold standard around the world, pundits of the reason why fraud occurs were not satisfied with Cressey as an absolute construct for fraudster motives. Many researchers have expounded and built on Cressey's theory. One such construct that expanded on Cressey's theory was the Diamond theory of fraud. Sorunke (2016) acknowledged that the Fraud Diamond Theory (FDT) was developed by David T. Wolfe and Dana R. Hermanson to add a component that Cressey may not have entertained in his theoretical framework of why fraudsters scheme companies out of their resources. Sorunke (2016) continued in his argument that both Wolfe and Hermanson strongly believed that the Cressey Fraud Triangle theory needed enhancement to improve both fraud prevention and detection. As a result, they presented an additional element to the one mentioned in the FTT–capability. The introduction of this variable by Wolfe and Hermanson reformulated FTT to what is known as the Fraud Diamond Theory (FDT). Cressey's fraud triangle was supported and used by audit regulators ASB and IAASB. Dissenters have argued that the model cannot solve the fraud challenge alone because two sides of the fraud triangle, rationalization and pressure, cannot be easily observed although they may be present (Sorunke,

2016). According to Sorunke (2016), Wolfe and Hermerson's (2004) definition of capability or skills is the ability, money, and recognition for committing a fraudulent action where there is an open door with an excellent opportunity, not only once, but many times. In RNPOs, this may be true for volunteers or administrators who have free access to monies or resources that are easily assessable.

Other Theories of Why Perpetrators Commit Fraud

Several of Cressey's contemporaries have provided additional explanations to why people commit fraudulent acts against organizations and financial crimes beyond the rationale afforded by the Fraud Triangle (Dorminey et al., 2012). One such theory that is appropriate to this study of leadership inability to detect and deter fraud in RNPOs in New Jersey is the Fraud scale theory. Albrecht et al. (1984) examined 212 incidences of fraud to determine if the same psychological traits exist with fraudsters. Dorminey et al. (2012) expounded that Dr. Albrecht and his colleagues Howe and Romney acknowledged Cressey's explanation of perpetrators of fraud behavior of pressure and opportunity, but they replace rationalization with personal integrity. Solomon (2003) described personal integrity as possessing the ability to close outside influences and temptations that are opposed to that what is good and wholesome.

Fraud Scale Theory

The fraud scale theory presents the argument that when situational pressures, perceived opportunities and personal integrity are high, occupational fraud is less likely to occur. Albrecht et al. (1984) described situational forces as when an individual has environmental stressors such as financial loss or high personal debt (ACFE, 2019b; Dorminey et al., 2012).

Figure 3

The Fraud Scale

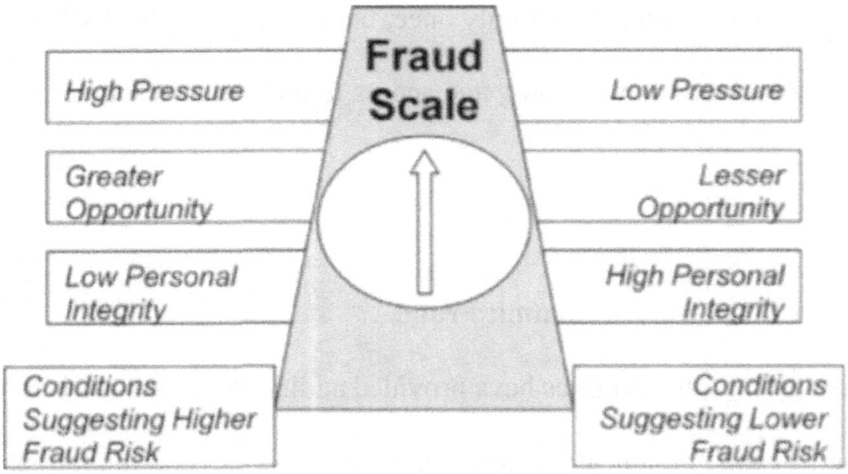

Adapted from Association of Certified Fraud Examiners. (2019b). *Fighting Fraud in Government*, p. 11.

This theory perhaps would be best described by why many RNPOs pastors, imams, and church administrators may have financial stressors and for various reasons may not be driven to steal from their organizations. The primary reason is they have high personal integrity, which would forbid them from defrauding their organization. Also, their 'fear of God' may be the guiding principle that governs them. However, some administrators are as the Bible states 'are hirelings that do not care for the flock' or the institution they serve and the 'fear of God' may be only a phrase to them and they unconscionably steal resources and monies from RNPOs they are supposed to serve.

Agency Theory

Outside of the previously mentioned theories, one of the rudimentary explanations of why perpetrators swindle their employers of their resources is the agency theory. Agency theory is one of the foremost theories in the economic study of organizations and management; however, its application is multidisciplinary (Pouryousefi & Frooman, 2019; Ross, 1973). Fundamentally, a principal-agent model involves a transaction between two parties. The principal party designs and prescribes the terms of a contract, making a designated offer to the other party–the agent. Pouryousefi and Frooman (2019) continued:

> The contract constitutes the implicit or explicit agreement of the terms of the interaction between the two parties. If the terms of the contract are agreed upon, the agent is supposed to carry out a service on behalf of the principal and in return, receive some compensation. Principals are, by definition, assumed to have the bargaining power to dictate the terms of the contract. The principal's task is to design a compensation scheme that attracts a sufficiently capable agent and efficiently motivates her to deliver high-quality services. (p. 3)

Issues arise with the principal-agency relationship, better known as agency problems, when after an agreement is consummated and differences arise between the principal expectation and the agent's actions (Machado & Gartner, 2018). One of the most significant challenges in organizations is information is asymmetric and principals are often not fully aware of what agents are doing (Gerard & Weber, 2014). The result is agents may conduct themselves contradictory to the terms they agreed to with the principal. The agency theory sprinkles all three elements of Cressey's theory. Agent motive is self-centered and finds an opportunity to take advantage of a situation contrary to what the principal ascribes. Dion (2016) purported agents are opportunist from either philosophical (Smith) egoism, or Machiavelli's philosophy. Dion (2016) borrowed from Smith that people by nature are selfish and that 'Nature' has given humankind a very weak spark of altruism and egoism must be controlled, whereas Machiavelli's philosophy states that people make choices because of fear of repercussions, and they primarily make individual decisions to protect 'self.'

In either case, although the agency theory focuses on shareholders and for-profit companies, the reality is human behavior is the same in RNPOs, and the aforementioned actions can easily happen in a mosque, church, or any religious institution that performs community services. Hence, administrators of these organizations cannot diminish that the mission does not make them exempt from self-loathing and selfish behaviors.

Motivated Reasoning Theory

The Motivated Reasoning Theory provides an equally important reason why fraudsters behave so atrociously towards RNPOs who perform such benevolent communal acts in their communities (Gramling & Schneider, 2018; Kunda, 1990). Motivated reasoning theory suggests that specific preferences primarily influence auditors' individual judgments and decisions. Auditors' decisions unconsciously are in part affected by their preferences even though they should make objective and impartial decisions (Gramling & Schneider, 2018). The motivated reason theory continues that auditors tend to make self-serving decisions that support their employers/clients' positions rather than real ones. In sum, the theory suggests that when the internal auditor is evaluating a process-specific control, the internal auditor will be less likely to assess that control as a material weakness when top management has primary influence over the internal audit function (IAF) than when the audit committee has central authority over the IAF (Gramling & Schneider, 2018, p. 323). There are a couple of implications with this theory in RNPOs. The first is because the argument is couched in all three FTTs of opportunity, motivation, and rationalization fraudsters, especially a skilled one may view this as an opportunity to commit fraud. The auditor's bias towards management may constituent as a motive to commit fraud, and rationalization of the auditors may present an opportunity for perpetrators to take advantage of the entity. The other implication of this theory is whether it is an internal or external auditor that management of RNPOS may be between the proverbial rock and hard place because if others are in collusion with the auditor to scheme the RNPOs or Faith Based Organizations(FBOs), then management may not recognize losses until long after the fraud is committed.

MICE Theory

A seminal explanation of why people commit fraud against organizations is the MICE or money, ideology, coercion and ego or entitlement theory (Rodgers et al., 2015). Kranacher et al. (2011) purported

> The *money*, *ideology*, *coercion*, and *ego/entitlement* (M.I.C.E.) model modifies the *non-sharable financial pressure* leg of the fraud triangle by expanding the list of possible fraud motivators beyond solely financial incentives. *Ideology* is usually associated with fraud schemes related to tax evasion and terrorism financing for which ideological beliefs are the driving impetus as opposed to personal financial difficulties. *Coercion* explains fraud schemes committed by individuals who are reluctantly pressured by others to collude and participate in the crime. Finally, *ego/entitlement* refers to fraud motivators related to someone's personality rather than his financial needs. (p. 875)

This model provides both financial and nonfinancial reasons why volunteers of RNPOs tend to commit fraud against their organization. The most obvious is the need for money. The next reason administrators may not consider is some people use religious corporations or similar types of organizations that are exempt from federal income tax under section 501(c)(3) of Title 26 of the

United States Code as a perfect cover to disguise incendiary activities to carry out their devious behavior, including stealing or diverting funds from these organization to fund terrorism. The third reason is where an innocent employee or volunteer in RNPOs is influenced by someone who may have supervisory power.

Table 2

Summary of Behavioral Theories of Fraud

Researcher	Topic
Cressey (1953)	Fraud Triangle Theory
Wolfe and Hermanson (1984)	Diamond Theory
Albrecht, Howe, and Romney (1984)	Fraud Scale Theory
Ross 1973	Agency Theory
Kunda (1990	Motivated Reasoning Theory
Kranacher, Riley, &Wells (2011)	Money, ideology, Coercion, Ego

Ideal Accounting Practices in RNPOs and Regulatory Oversight

Accounting in RNPOs varies depending on the size complexity and personnel expertise within each organization. Harris et al. (2017) found evidence the more complex charitable organizations are, the more likely they are to experience internal control challenges. As a result, more complex charities are faced with more substantial asset diversions. Harris et al. (2017) continued based on prior research complexity is viewed as the number of "different revenue sources reported by the charity, including donations, government grants, and/or program service revenue (i.e., tuition, ticket sales, etc.)" (p. 156). Despite the size or complexity of the organization, various regulatory and accounting oversight bodies have outlined recommendations for ideal accounting practices for not for profit organizations. Accounting practices should provide clarity to stakeholders and strengthen not-for-profit financial reporting, which include stopping or reducing fraud (Fitzsimons et al., 2018). The following are the guidelines that not for profits can use to assist them in their accounting practices.

- Revises the net asset classification scheme to two classes (net assets with donor restrictions and net assets without donor restrictions) instead of the previous three.
- Enhances disclosures for self-imposed limits on the use of resources without donor-imposed restrictions and the composition of net assets with donor restrictions.
- Updates the accounting and disclosure requirements for underwater endowment funds.
- Requires net presentation of investment expenses against investment return on the statement of activities and eliminates the requirement to disclose investment expenses that have been netted.
- Requires the presentation of expenses by nature as well as function, including an analysis of expenses showing the relationship between functional and natural classification for all expenses.
- Requires qualitative disclosures on how a not-for-profit manages its available liquid resources.
- Requires quantitative disclosures that communicate the availability of financial assets to meet cash needs for general expenditures within one year of the balance sheet date.
- Allows for a choice between the direct and indirect method of reporting operating cash flows; presentation of the indirect reconciliation is no longer required if using the direct method. (FASB, p. 1)

The FASB is not the only regulatory agency that has proposed ideal accounting practices for NPOs. Harris et al. (2017) pointed out that the IRS requires NPOs or charities to disclose information about their awareness of any asset diversion and their governance structures. Also, the

IRS requires tax-exempt charitable organizations that receive more than $25,000 in revenue to complete IRS Form 990. As part of this form, whether organizations are museums, churches, or trade unions, they must answer the following questions since the filing of their last Form 990. The questions includes 'what is the size and independence of the organization's board of directors' and "any members of the board of directors have family relationships with any other member, officer, or key employees, and whether any significant changes have been made to its organization" (Donnelly, 2010, p. 183).

In addition to that IRS regulations, "Section 4958 applies to all organizations exempt under IRC sections 501(c)(3) (other than private foundations) and 501(c)(4). IRC §4958 proscribes 'excess benefit transactions' between certain charitable organizations and "disqualified persons" (generally, those in a position to exercise 'substantial influence' over the organization)" (Tushe, 2016, p. 67).

Regulatory oversight has taken place on a federal level. Also, some state governments were concerned with some of the nonprofit financial abuses and fraud so they have implemented their regulatory requirements and accounting standards. The State of New York is one of the leaders in nonprofits, including RNPOs oversight, implementing the Revitalization Act (Tushe, 2016). New York legislators attempted through the Act to modernize outdated provisions, improve accountability, and strengthen board independence (Tushe, 2016). To ensure independence and objectivity of the board and its director, New York legislators made it illegal for one person to lead both the administration and governance of the organization and shifted the responsibility between multiple parties who work in tandem (Tushe, 2016). Another provision of the law states that a nonprofit entity with an annual income over $500,000 must create an audit committee composed solely of independent directors (Tushe, 2016).

Finally, one of the provisions of the Revitalization Act is it reduces some audit-related items related to financial reporting with the Attorney General for nonprofits. In addition, Tushe (2016) pointed out that New York legislators require nonprofit corporations receiving gross revenue and support greater than $500,000 in a fiscal year are required to file an annual financial report and an audit report prepared by an independent CPA with the Attorney General. Through the IRS Form 990, all of FASB's recommendations and various state regulations may not apply to all the smaller or medium size RNPOs, the questions that IRS form 990 asks, and some of the regulatory bodies and state laws can be used as a template by financial administrators of RNPOs in their plight to detect and deter fraudulent activities.

Fraud in Not for Profits

There were approximately 1.56 to 1.9 million nonprofits registered with the IRS in 2015 and contributed almost $1 trillion to the U.S. economy in 2015, constituting 5.4% of the country's gross domestic product (Donnelly, 2010; McKeever, 2019; Tushe, 2016). Donnelly (2010) acknowledged that the IRS approves an average of 182 organizations every day, which includes Saturdays, Sundays, and federal holidays. One of the challenges is all organizations are vulnerable to the threat of fraud (Harris et al., 2017; Stephens & Flaherty, 2013). The reality is fraud is approximately one-sixth of all the major embezzlements that occur in the nonprofit industry. Shaharuddin and Sulaiman (2015) pointed out that even though religious organizations and mosques are regarded as 'sacred' and people who worked there are perceived to have high moral values, the increase in financial scandals, like the misappropriation of funds, amongst these institutions are brought about by poor accounting and internal control practices. Shaharuddin and Sulaiman (2015) identified several factors that have contributed to fraud in RNPOs. One of the factors that Shaharuddin and Sulaiman (2015) identified as an impediment of accounting practices in RNPOS or religious organization is the dichotomy between what is considered sacred and secular. Concrete examples do not altogether support the sacred versus secular ideology as it pertains to accounting in RNPOs (Jacob, 2005 as cited in Shaharuddin & Sulaiman, 2015). Research suggests that Islamic organizations and some churches prefer accounting activities to be undertaken by accountants with some religious connections. Another challenge within RNPOs is immense trust in personnel (Shaharuddin & Sulaiman, 2015; Sulaiman et al., 2008). The lack of a healthy dose of mistrust or misplaced trust has created gaps and internal control problems in RNPOs. The lack of supervision has provided fraudsters the opportunity to victimize RNPOs of millions of dollars (Shaharuddin & Sulaiman, 2015).

Another variable that exists within RNPOS that affects their ability to detect and deter fraud, is the lack of involved owners (Shaharuddin & Sulaiman, 2015). Unlike corporations and the other forms of business models, RNPOs do not have stockholders who always scrutinize the corporations' books to determine how their investments are performing. Religious-based organizations such as mosques, churches, and temples are among organization's models which generally lack transparency and accountability to their donors, some stakeholders, and the public (Shaharuddin & Sulaiman, 2015).

Another determinant that can contribute to fraud is the involvement of unskilled volunteers in RNPOs (Ventura & Daniel, 2010). It is not surprising there are improper accounting practices and weak internal controls in religious organizations because many volunteer treasurers on accounting matters are inadequately trained (Shaharuddin & Sulaiman, 2015). Unfortunately, the ingredients mentioned earlier are a recipe for fraud and the reality of how some RNPOs run their accounting departments.

Overview and Role of RNPO Governance

Because of the misappropriation of hundreds of millions of dollars, accountability to stakeholders and transparency has become an unpleasant fact in the nonprofit sector (Geer et al., 2008). Financial scandals, watchdog groups, tax-policy regulators, donors' bills of rights legislative reforms, and funding regulations have placed nonprofit organizations in the limelight. Geer et al. (2008) acknowledged that some nonprofit administrators are uncertain about how to manage and develop accountability within their institutions.

RNPOs are top down organizations that are run by pastors' imams, rabbis, and administrators with the purpose of carrying out a mission on behalf of multiple stakeholders. Each administrator, board of trustee member, and executive normally adopt or fail to adopt a certain effective leadership style or a combination of leadership styles to manage their entity (Bernstein et al., 2016). The principle -agency theory that good governance includes and is not limited to the management of systems and processes ensuring the overall accountability, control, and directions of the organization (Cornforth & Brown, 2014). Bernstein et al. (2016) continued that practitioner's literature viewpoint of good governance places the burden of administrators to fulfill the legal and fiduciary responsibilities including: (a) oversight of programs and services; (b) financial, ethical, and legal oversight; (c) fundraising; (d) outreach setting the organization's mission and purpose; (e) selecting, supporting, and evaluating the chief executive; (f) strategic planning; and (g) recruiting of new board members. The board of directors as the peak of the governance structure in NPO and those who are stewards have the ultimate responsibility for the effectiveness of the entities they serve (Harris et al., 2017; Jensen, 2003). Board monitoring involves regular oversight to ensure the organization has adequate resources and systems to continue accountability to its various stakeholders (Harris et al., 2017; Jensen, 2003).

Harris et al. (2017) reasoned that board or administrative oversight can mitigate the likelihood of asset diversions in a couple of ways. First, periodic reviews of mission-related activities and financial reports enables leaders of RNPOs to detect potential problems sooner. Second, monitoring allows administrators in these organizations to determine if there are gaps in their internal control system.

However, governance in not for profits organizations is layered by the board of directors, the CEO, and in some cases they are the administrative leadership which can include volunteers. Whereas, in other cases the pastors, imams, or the spiritual leaders are also the administrative leaders in RNPOs. Larger institutions that are more organized may have a dedicated financial employee or volunteer to monitor the financial records of the organization.

Types of Leadership

Nonetheless, the success of RNPOs' ability to detect and deter fraud in their organizations in part or stated by some pundits in whole hinges on the leadership style or combination of styles the organization adopts. Sankaran et al. (2014) offered a working definition of leadership as a person's capability that transcends the standard scope of operational management to include a strategic capacity and the ability to deal with difficulty. The individual or individuals also has/have attributes such as innovation and vision, as well as a defensible confidence in using these attributes in an organizational role. Sankaran et al. (2014) identified capability as a necessity of good leadership as "mastery over a range of tasks or functions acquired through experience (professional and personal) and training (formal and informal)" (p. 556). Sankaran et al. (2014) continued 'capability' is differentiated from 'competency' in that it is viewed as the ability to undertake a range of tasks or functions, whereas capability is seen as "a meta-competency that weaves the relevant competencies, experience and knowledge into a coherent set of behaviors" (p. 556).

Tone at the Top Leadership. There is an abundance of academic literature about leadership styles. One of the styles that pundits of organizational leadership have embraced is the tone at the top leadership model. The tone at the top model is cradled in the self-concept maintenance construct which suggests individuals are torn between competing stimulus. The dichotomy with this model is people are caught between achieving benefit by misrepresenting data versus maintaining a positive self-concept by reporting data accurately as individuals possess a range of dishonest behavior they may act on (Pickerd et al., 2015). Mazar et al. (2008) continued that two variables determine a 'magnitude range of dishonesty.' The first is the degree of focus individuals' pay to their own standards of conduct such as religious norms, and the second which somewhat hinges on Cressey's viewpoint of rationalizations, is the degree to which people categorize their actions into more likeminded terms and find explanations for their actions. Unethical behavior becomes acceptable in an organization to the point actions can be rationalized by employees and volunteers in the entity (Mazar et al., 2008; Pickerd et al., 2015).

In sum, tone of the top leadership is a culture of integrity, control consciousness, and ethical "values from upper-level management and the board of directors, which is traditionally thought to influence and promote ethical decision making by mid- and lower-level employees (Pickerd et al., 2015, p. 80; Schaubroeck et al., 2012). Pickerd et al. (2015) pointed out that because of the overwhelming anecdotal and empirical evidence, tone at the top construct is well recognized and embraced by business leaders, governments, professional organizations, and accounting researchers due to the fact that strong tone at the top provides companies financial reporting and operational benefits. RNPOs can deter fraud by setting a staunch tone at the top. Although it may not be a magic bullet, the evidence suggests that leadership in organizations who sets an ethical tempo show volunteers and employees most likely will follow.

Competency Based Leadership. The competency based leadership construct was first coined by Boyatzis (1982). An effective manager or leader is one who possess certain competencies that enables them to attain success in their job. Success refers to desired outcomes (Boyatzis, 1982). Boyatzis (2008) expounded that there are three competencies superior performers possess. First, supervisor performers have emotional intelligence competency or the ability to understand, recognize and use emotional information about themselves to produce superior performance. Second, one of the competencies outstanding performers possess is cognitive intelligence competency, which is the ability to analyze information that produces effective performance. The third competency is social intelligence competency, which is the ability to discern and use emotional information about others that leads to supervisor performance.

Sanz and Fontrodona (2019) and Morales-Sánchez and Cabello-Medina (2015) provided a more contemporary literature perspective of many competencies in relation to cognitive skills, such as personal involvement, analytical capacity, teamwork, motivation, initiative, interpersonal skills, communication, and leadership. Sanz and Fontrodona (2019) continued that some of these competencies have a more moral overtone and individuals that possess them do not only contribute to the performance of a task, but primarily move the individual to a higher good and to a higher degree of fulfillment. Morales-Sánchez and Cabello-Medina (2015) asserted that moral competence can be defined as that skill set, knowledge, abilities, and attitudes attained through experience, which enable employees in the engagement of ethical behaviors in a specific job virtue.

RNPOs who employ leaders who possess the above-mentioned competencies, especially the moral one, would most likely deter fraud because of the lens through which these leaders view their roles.

Servant Leadership. Some leadership styles lends itself to good ethical organization culture. In recent decades, servant leadership model was adopted by some practitioners as one of the models that seeks the good of the organization rather than self-interest. Pulumbo (2016) suggested that servant leaders in theory are innately motivated in aiding employees and volunteers in fulfilling their organizational duties opposed to the pursuit of self-interest within the organization. Lumpkin and Achen (2018) purported that companies like Southwest Airlines have adopted servant leadership approach. The servant leadership model uses as its premise ethical conduct among its foundational themes where self-described servant-leaders choose to serve others first, through dedication, caring, showing empathy to, trusting others, and nurture the development of leadership abilities in others (Spears, 2010). Palumbo (2016) identified 10 traits that servant leaders

1. Listening - leaders actively listens to no verbal and verbal communication reflecting on the meaning of the information and paying attention to one's inner voice.
2. Healing - A determination to help heal relationship with others and simultaneously working on healing themselves.
3. Empathy - motivated to understand and empathize with others.
4. Persuasion - oppose to use coercion servant leaders seek to persuade others in making decisions.
5. Awareness - have the self-awareness of the ethics, power and values of an organization.

6. Conceptualization - possess the optics examine and solve organizational wide issues. Servant leaders dream beyond the day to day realities.
7. Foresight - possessing the ability and the intuition the likely outcome of the likely outcome of a situation based on understanding the past and present.
8. Building community - servant leaders are committed in building a sense of community in their organization.
9. Stewardship - psychologically embracing that as a leader they hold the trust of resources for the greater good of others.
10. Commitment to the growth of people - servant leaders view the development of employees as an important asset and their growth as paramount importance.

Other theorist of the servant leader model viewed servant leaders to have varying attributes to Spears construct (Russell & Stone, 2002). Pulumbo (2016) distilled servant leadership trait into two categories. Inner traits or functional attributes and accompanying traits as the leader ability to interact with followers (Russell & Stone, 2002). Pulumbo (2016) continued that "functional attributes embrace a farsighted vision that makes the leader able to anticipate the unforeseeable; strong honesty; integrity; trust; modeling; pioneering; and the desire to serve, appreciate, and empower the followers" (p. 85). Pulumbo (2016) continued that accompanying attributes "include communication, credibility, competence, visibility, stewardship, encouragement, listening, teaching, influence, encouragement, and delegation" (p. 85). More contemporary literature of servant leadership is needed (van Dierendonck, 2011). Pulumbo (2016) reinterpreted the fundamental attributes of servant leadership, which includes six fundamental areas: (a) humility, (b) stewardship, (c) willingness of developing and empowering people, (d) authenticity, (e) ability to provide effective direction, and (f) stewardship.

Barbuto and Wheeler (2006) offered a five-dimensional aspect of servant leadership theory with an emphasis that ideal a servant leader is generally inspired by an altruistic calling and possesses an innate desire to produce a positive difference in others' lives. Servant leaders are concerned with persuasive mapping or encouraging followers to visualize the future (Barbuto & Wheeler, 2006). Stewardship or community development is an emotional healing or an organizational environment that is safe for the followers. Wisdom is the ability to anticipate external contingencies.

Barbuto and Wheeler (2006) purported servant leadership promoted several beneficial outcomes in organizations that are desirable, especially in RNPOs such as altruistic traits of leaders, lower staff turnover rates, strong organizational commitment which RNPOs prefer because it promotes the good of the organization above individual selfish needs. Pulumbo (2016) found that servant leadership tends to promote dependency behavior by following and when the leader was absent followers tend to feel disempowered.

Spiritual Intelligence Leadership. There are some leadership models that align with RNPOs and its organizational culture. A couple of models that are akin to RNPOs culture are servant and spiritual intelligent leadership (Gardner, 2000; Qadri et al., 2017). Effective goal achieving abilities, managerial decision-making skills, personal meaning production and an introduction of self-existence awareness such as emotional and spiritual management are critical competencies for leaders (Öksüz & Ker-Dinçer, 2012; Qadri et al., 2017; Rana et al., 2017). Vaughan (2002) acknowledged spiritual intelligence leadership has three fundamental components. First, leaders must have the awareness or soul, or the creative life force of the evolution. Second, leaders must possess the inner life of spirit and mind in relation to their connection to the world. Third, managers must be capable of a high level of consciousness and deep comprehension of existential issues. According to Zohar (2005), spiritual intelligence is the need by proponents of this type of intelligence to attain the deeper meanings, higher values, more fundamental purposes in life, and the vision that inspires us to lead lives of greater meaning.

Zohar (2005) concluded that leaders can develop spiritually intelligent traits by consciously incorporating the following 12 ideologies:

1. Self-awareness: is awareness of the authentic self that connect to the deeper things in the universe.
2. Spontaneity: possessing the poise to appropriately respond in the moment
3. Vision and value-led: Living with the aspiration and deep beliefs of making the world a better place or making a difference in the world.
4. Holistic: Leaders' ability to understand that everything is intricately interwoven and making the relationships, and connections to the bigger picture; each person can make a difference in the whole picture.
5. Celebration of diversity: Embracing the differences of everyone inside and outside of one's circle.
6. Compassion: possessing the quality of deep feeling or empathy even for enemies.
7. Field independence: Standing up for one beliefs or convictions. The willingness to go against the crowd or group think.
8. Sense of vocation: A feeling that a person is called by God to serve.
9. Humility: Having the understanding as a leader there are other voices in the larger picture and as leader one can be wrong in his or her viewpoint.

10. Propensity to ask "Why?" Questions: Spiritual intelligent leaders ask the hard questions why to obtain a better understand of things.
11. Positive use of adversity: here leaders own, acknowledge, and recognize mistakes and things that they did wrong.
12. Ability to reframe: The ability to stand back and view a situation from the lens of the bigger picture.

In an ever meta-organization environment that requires leaders to possess particular traits, spiritual intelligent leadership can enhance a leader's ability in RNPOs to deal with the potential threat of fraud by employees and volunteers in their organizations. Leaders can also look at the bigger picture as Zohar (2005) contended to deal with the inner egos that may cause management to steal valuable resources from RNPOs they serve.

Overview of Detection and Deterrence Methods

Religious not for profit organizations are complex entities because of the diversity of backgrounds of the people they serve and the choice of leadership styles that leaders choose to incorporate. Perpetrators who steal organization's resources or commit fraud are multifarious ingenious beings who can devise strategies to obtain an advantage over others by false representations, which makes the incorporation of deterrent methods by entities extremely important to the overall success of detecting and deterring fraud (Webster, 2019). To detect fraud, Kummer et al. (2015) found in their research that entities often utilize specific fraud assessment instruments and/or policies. Leaders of any organization through a fraud assessment will find that there are an assortment of fraud detection and prevention tools available to them.

COSO Framework and Internal Controls

Quintessential of all tools available to management in deterring and detecting fraud is an effective internal control system. Internal control is the functioning management tool to reduce risk by eliminating errors and identifying fraud inside an entity (Lakis & Giriunas, 2012). There are several other benefits to management that the concept of internal control was "presented for the first time in 1949 by the American Institute of Certificated Accountants (AICPA)" (Lakis & Giriunas, 2012, para. 3). Lakis and Giriunas (2012) identified that the AICPA defined internal control as a plan and other coordinated efforts and ways by which an organization uses to protect and keep safe its assets, check the secrecy and reliability of data, and ensure management policies are upheld (D'Aquila, 2013). Frazier (2016) highlighted that in 1992 The Committee of Sponsoring Organizations of the Treadway Commission (COSO) formalized an integrated holistic framework for enterprises, perhaps representing the first major formal comprehensive attempt to address the lack of proper internal controls and provide a design to assist organizations with fraud. This model was a template and an all-inclusive standard for measurement and a prelude to the Sarbanes-Oxley Act (SOX). Specifically, section 404 of the SOX act provided how to establish and maintain internal controls over financial reporting. The COSO framework is by and large, according to some practitioners and pundits, one of the most comprehensive summaries of an effective internal control system necessary to strengthen efficiency within the management of any enterprise (Frazier, 2016). It expanded on AICPA's definition of internal controls introducing controls are not only concerned with accounting mistakes, but also involves the implementation of a means of the prevention of mistakes and the deterrence of fraud.

The COSO framework is one of the best templates that entities can utilize in its effort to detect and deter fraudulent behavior. D'Aquila (2013) continued that because of the comprehensive nature of the COSO Framework, Securities Exchange Commission (SEC) along with Public Accounting Oversight Board (PCOAB) highlighted the importance of internal control as part of its regulation. The SEC final rule stated, "The COSO Framework satisfies our criteria and may be used as an evaluation framework for purposes of management's annual internal control evaluation and disclosure requirement." The PCOAB stated that in AS 2 of its policies that the organization recognized the COSO framework as the ideal framework when management evaluates the effectiveness of internal control over financial reporting and when auditors perform audits of internal control over financial reporting.

In response to the challenges faced by not for profit organizations and government entities, in 2013 the Committee of Sponsoring Organizations (COSO) published its revised publication of the Internal Control–Integrated Framework (IC Framework; D'Aquila & Houmes, 2014). The revised framework held to the initial definition of internal control and its five attributes, which are (a) risk assessment, (b) information and communication, (c) control environment, (d) control activities, and (e) monitoring along with its three aims which are operations, reporting, and compliance. However, opposed from the original framework, the new framework introduced distinct control components into explicitly stated attributes and principles along with explicit internal control for information technology (D'Aquila & Houmes, 2014; Janvrin et al., 2012). The basic tenets of the COSO framework are as follows

1. Risk assessment - the identification and analysis of risks relevant to the achievement of objectives.
2. Information and communication - is the pertinent internal and external information that must be identified, captured, and communicated within an organization that enable people to carry out their responsibilities. In the new COSO framework it also identifies

information systems that produces reports of operational, financial, and compliance-related information that make it possible to run and control the business

3. Control activities - are management directives or activities designed to dissuade theft and fraudulent activities such as verifications, approvals, reconciliations, authorizations, reviews of operating performance, the segregation of duties and the safeguarding of assets.
4. Control environment - it is the foundational premise that sets the enterprise tempo and consciousness providing the discipline, structure, operating style, integrity, ethical values, employee competence, management's philosophy and, and the leadership provided by senior management and the board of directors.
5. Monitoring - is the activity that organizations incorporates with their regular management and supervisory activities as well as other actions that personnel undertake while performing their duties.

On September 6, 2017, after two years of deliberations, COSO released its Enterprise Risk Management: Integrating Strategy and Performance in attempt to update its framework to enhance the value received from Enterprise Risk Management (ERM) programs (Pierce & Goldstein, 2018). Pierce and Goldstein (2018) continued that COSO released their Enterprise Risk Management to revise its draft of the 2004 Enterprise Risk Management—Integrated Framework. The revision was designed to destroy the barriers and segregated treatment of the two processes of risk management and strategic planning (Pierce & Goldstein, 2018). The new model introduced objective setting and risk response to its core tenets of the framework. COSO framework viewed objective setting as high level goals or strategies that the organization desires to pursue and risk response is the alternative steps enterprises consider for responding to the identified risk (Pierce & Goldstein, 2018). COSO (2017) stated

> by integrating Enterprise Risk Management with strategy-setting, an organization gains insight into the risk profile associated with strategy and the business objectives. Doing so guides the organization and helps to sharpen the strategy and the tasks necessary to carry it out. (p. 45)

In sum "an entity can enhance its overall performance by integrating Enterprise Risk Management into day-to-day operations and more closely linking business objectives to risk" (COSO, 2017, p. 5). Frazier (2016) pointed out that internal controls are not without flaws and small entities are challenges with the implementation of an effective internal control systems because of various limitations such as the size of its staff and costs and other constraints. The reality is some type of internal controls system is still possible at little or no cost and is better than no internal control system at all.

There are several benefits to internal controls (Frazer, 2016). Suárez (2017) contended that internal controls can assist organizations with controlling unnecessary costs. Frazer (2016) argued that preventable internal controls can assist an enterprise in their planning of what costs can be reduced and what costs are absolutely necessary in its day to day operations. Another benefit of internal controls is they know which transactions have been validated and recorded properly in the maintenance and preparation of financial statements (Frazer, 2016). Preventative internal controls are used by management to eliminate and minimize any question irregularities and errors that may occur within an organization's business practices (Galloway, 2003 as cited in Frazer, 2016). One preventative control measure is the division of labor. Companies have separation of duties to ensure that assets are protected and proprietary information is not breached. In broader sense, internal controls systems are not only accounting and financial in nature but include inventory controls, administrative and managerial controls, cash controls, purchasing controls, sales statistics, and budget preparation (Rutherford & O'Fallon, 2007 as cited in Frazer, 2016). Financial and accounting controls are primarily concerned with the assurance that all the financial statements such as the balance sheet, cash flow statements, retained earnings, and income statements, are reliable and properly maintained for use by the management.

Frazer (2016) contended that internal controls are not without flaws. Frazer (2016) pointed out family businesses and collusion by employees could circumvent internal control. Frazer (2016) continued that employee turnover, the stability and capacity of a business, vulnerabilities to human error, carelessness, misunderstandings, and tight budgets are all factors that could undermine internal controls. RNPO administrators, depending on the size and complexity, are faced with all of the aforementioned vulnerabilities with their internal control system and can benefit from the advantage of a properly implemented and maintained internal control system.

Code of Conduct Policy and Ethic/Fraud Training

Apart from internal control system, there are other fraud deterrent tools available to management to thwart would be schemers from pilfering organizations' assets. One of the tools available to management is establishing a code of conduct and ethics training. Many RNPOs assume that because many of their volunteers and employees are high character people. People join organizations for various reasons and not all have high character. To create an even playing field, management of RNPOs can design a code of conduct policy and engage their employees and volunteers in ethics training. Nawawi and Salin (2018) submitted that a code of conduct is a written document that is designed to ensure that all employees, vendors, or agents of an organization conduct their business within the framework of the company's policies and procedures as well as all applicable federal and local laws and regulations. Nawawi and Salin (2018) found that documented policies such as a robust code of conduct policies and procedures, acts as a foundation of internal control and needs to be implemented in all major aspects of any company's business. Nawawi and Salin (2018) continued that such polices must be regularly reviewed and updated to safeguard that all the documents remain effective and continue to support the organization's business activities. Code of conduct documents serve as a guideline for employees, dealers, volunteers, suppliers, contractors, and vendors to carry out their routine jobs in the workplace and with external parties and assist with key issues, such as bribery, conflicts of interest, insider trading, and data integrity to name a few. Nawawi and Salin (2018) concluded such policies can be critical tools in the prevention and minimization of losses from fraud and can protect the entities from misuse by those with criminal motives.

However, the document is only as effective if employees, vendors, suppliers, and volunteers understand its content. Nawawi and Salin (2018) found that in their study that some employees who violated the code of conduct policies knew it existed and even read the documents, but they did not understand its contents. Johnson and Wright (2004) contended that one of the most important variables that impacts whether an employee will report a questionable act is the existence of a comprehensive code of ethics coupled with regular training of the code of ethics in the organization. This policy should be reviewed with employees annually because it otherwise would most likely be disregarded (Johnson & Wright, 2004). For an organization to be successful in their attempt to discourage fraudsters, employees need to understand what wrongful acts are (Johnson & Wright, 2004). Four conditions must exist for a wrongful act to exist:

1. The employees must believe that the act is wrong.
2. The employee must believe that the act is serious to merit reporting to supervisors or enforcing agents of the enterprise.

3. The individual must believe that the wrongful act occurred or is occurring. and
4. The individual must believe that they have a responsibility to report the malfeasance (Johnson & Wright, 2004).

Johnson and Wright (2004) pointed out as it pertains to internal controls when employees are trained about the purpose of rule such as cosigner, realize that if a check was written it would help employees understand the purpose of the internal controls, which in turn can help deter fraud. Finally, employee training is a critical defense and reminds employees, vendors, and suppliers that fraud impacts everyone in the organization and reporting fraud or illegal activities can mitigate losses to an organization (Johnson & Wright, 2004). RNPOs are no exception to creating and implementing a code of ethics and training of what it means. Though RNPOs most likely would have high character volunteers and employees, the reality is that not everyone has the right motives. In addition, there may be a trigger such as large student debt or chronic unemployment in a person's life who works for a RNPOs that may cause them to commit fraud.

Identifying Red Flags. Internal control systems have gaps and are not perfect. Thus it is incumbent that employees and management understand various types of red flags or warning signals of fraud in detecting fraud (Kramer, 2015). One area that may be advantageous to organizations in unmasking the blight of fraud is training employees how to spot red flags. Dal Magro and Da Cunha (2017) defined red flags as mechanisms that can be used by enterprises for early assessing and the detection of possible fraud. Red flags are warning signals such as either personal characteristics of perpetrators, events, situational pressure, opportunities or combination of factors indicates a presence of potential fraud whether on behalf of the company itself or for any personal gain (Dal Magro & Roberto da Cunha, 2017; Mangala & Kumari, 2017). Most of the literature written are about behavioral red flags. However apart from behavioral red flags, there are internal operating procedural red flags (Tschakert et al., 2016). Dal Magro and Da Cunha (2017) acknowledged that reg flags can be categorized and divided into six groups: economic and financial situation, sector/industry, structure and environment, managers, financial reporting and external auditing. The ACFEs identified in its 2020 Report to the Nations on Occupational Fraud and Abuse that fraudsters may exhibit the following behavioral red flags (ACFE, 2019a; Tschakert et al., 2016).

The first behavioral trait fraudsters may display is a lifestyle where they are living beyond their means. Another behavioral sign is addiction problems. Fraudsters may have a gambling addiction, chemical addition, and other addictions that may trigger them to turn to fraud to obtain the funds to support their addictions. One of the primary reasons for fraud is financial difficulties. People who commit fraud often time are having difficulty paying their personal bills, forcing them to find a means to cover the difference in their bills. Another red flag that is common in fraudsters is they have a remarkably close association with customers or vendors. Perpetrators of fraud are often highly suspicious, irritable, and defensive in the smallest issues.

Fraudsters have control issues or an unwillingness to share duties, wheeler-dealer attitude involving shrewd or unscrupulous behavior, refuse to take vacations, complain about their lack of authority, increased smoking, make up excuses for missing documentation or shortages, and find scapegoats (Tschakert et al., 2016). Most offenders are under increased stress as they fear detection. Besides the ones already mentioned, the Association of Certified Fraud Examiners identified, 14 additional red flags that were common in 92% of all fraudsters, including: refusal to take vacation; social isolation; past legal problems; instability in life circumstances; past employment related issues with fraud; divorce/family problems; wheeler dealer attitude; excessive pressure within the organization; complaints about lack of authority; control issues; and unwillingness to share duties.

Non behavioral red flags depend upon on the fraud scheme and what area of the organization the fraudster has authority to manipulate key documents to in the organization for obtaining personal gain. Example of non-behavioral red flags are not limited to receiving invoices that are numbered consecutively from one customer, lack of normal fold marks in mailed check envelopes suggesting the items was not mailed, missing normal vendor information (such as a physical location or a phone number), and even-dollar amounts are some of the warning signs of a fictitious vendor schemes (Kramer, 2015).

SOX and Fraud Deterrence in Not for Profits. The intended target of the Sarbanes–Oxley act (SOX) was chiefly to private for-profit organizations and privately traded entities, however, certain provisions apply to all other private enterprises in the United States and around the world (Nezhina & Brudney, 2012; Saxton & Neely, 2019). Wilbanks (2016) identified 11 components of the SOX act:

1. Public Company Accounting Oversight Board;
2. Auditor Independence;
3. Corporate Responsibility;
4. Enhanced Financial Disclosures;
5. Analyst Conflicts of Interest;
6. Commission Resources and Authority;
7. Studies and Reports;
8. Corporate and Criminal Fraud Accountability;
9. White-Collar Crime Penalty Enhancement;

10. Corporate Tax Returns;

11. Corporate Fraud and Accountability.

Though SOX was a government policy meant to deter fraud in private for profit corporations and publicly traded companies because of mounting pressure by stakeholders for good governance and transparency, some aspects of SOX have trickled into the nonprofit sector (Saxton & Neely, 2019). Not for profits that implement at least two of the three SOX related written policies that are recommended for nonprofit organizations—record retention policies, conflict-of-interest policies, and whistleblower policies, saw better results detecting and deterring fraud in organizations (Saxton & Neely, 2019). Regarding record retention policies, SOX empowered Public Company Accounting Oversight Board (PCAOB) to establish records-retention standards and it primarily applies to the retention of documentation for incomplete audit engagements (for which no report was issued) and up to seven years after the cessation of audit work due to an auditor withdrawal or termination based on what the state or local government policies require. Ordinarily record retention is up to five years unless stated otherwise longer by local and state statutory and regulatory minimums. Some RNPO organizations may not have the volume of paperwork of their for -profits counterparts. A records retention would enable administrators and auditors to follow a paper trail to determine who may be involved in egregious acts in the organizations.

Whistle Blower Policy. Pundits, practitioners, and academia consider whistle blower policy as an integral part of corporate governance through revealing and alleviating fraud, corruption, and other forms of malfeasance in both the for profit and not for profit sector (Dixon, 2016; Miceli & Near, 1994; Saxton & Neely, 2019). Vandekerckhove (2018) acknowledged that the term *whistle blower* was initial coined by Ralph Nader in 1971, who defined it as the disclosure by enterprise's current or former employees, vendors, contractors of immoral, illegal, or illegitimate practices in the organization under the control of their employers to persons or organizations that may be able to effect action (Gao & Brink, 2017). Qusqas and Kleiner (2001) submitted that the term whistle blower is better known from a sporting event where the referee blows the whistle to identify to a player that an illegal or foul play took place. Smaili and Arroyo (2019) provided a simpler definition of whistle blower stating that a whistleblower is an actor who uses inside channels such as manager of the organizations or external agents such as government and regulatory agencies to disclose wrongdoing by internal or external fraudsters providing the whistleblowers intent is not tainted by dissent or entails loyalty conflicts. A 2016 publication by the Association of Certified Fraud Examiners where an analysis of more than 2410 cases of occupational fraud in more than 114 countries found 39.1% of fraud cases were detected by a whistleblower (ACFE, 2019a; Smaili & Arroyo, 2019). Smaili and Arroyo (2019) continued that whistle blowing was part of the SOX and was strengthen by the Dodd-Frank Wall Street and Consumer Protection Act which states audit committees must adopt procedures regarding "the confidential, anonymous submission by employees of the issuer of concerns regarding questionable accounting or auditing matters," thus providing some degree of protection for whistle blower from adverse repercussions from employers (p. 96). In older literature, whistle blowers were only considered internal or external. Current literature broadens the classification of whistleblowers to role-prescribed, self-interested, skeptical and protective whistle blowers (Smaili & Arroyo, 2019). Chen and Lai (2014) also provided whistleblowers into four conceptual types: rebel, indifferent, mature, and spoiled whistle blowers. Gao and Brink (2017) found that employees in organizations with idealistic ethical positions are more likely to disclose fraud. This is important because employees with narcissistic propensities may not be credible whistleblowers and the legitimacy of their claim may be dismissed.

Smaili and Arroyo (2019) presented the whistle blower triangle as more contemporaneous parallelism of the Cressey fraud triangle contending that whistleblowers have pressure, opportunity, and the rationalization of why they reveal that there is wrongdoing going on in their organization. Smaili and Arroyo (2019) posited that whistleblowers may have socio-psychological pressures such as religious conviction, morality, and values. Some of these moral values were likely instilled by parents and teachers of whistleblowers. Smaili and Arroyo (2019) continued that financial pressure, media notoriety, and professional goals may also be drivers of whistleblowers' intent to reveal that there is egregious behavior in an enterprise.

Opportunity relates to the resources within internal or external resources that can assist or protect the whistleblower. External and internal resources can include and may not be limited to compensation, anti-retaliation resources such as internal procedures, code of ethics, shareholder activism, legal protections, and corporate governance mechanisms (Smaili & Arroyo, 2019).
Smaili and Arroyo (2019) argued that rationalization is the reasoning justification process behind the whistleblowing decision to implicate themselves with wrongdoing in an organization. Whistleblowing is a difficult choice. Whistle blowers can opt to be silent for fear of the possible repercussions or choose to heed to their moral or religious beliefs to come forward with the knowledge of the wrongdoing in the enterprise. Smaili and Arroyo (2019) continued in their research that whistleblowing falls into two types of dissonance behavior. The first is the act of whistleblowing (behavior) and the cognizance that one's employment could be in jeopardy (cognition), and the second occurs when the individual decides to blow the whistle knowing that other stakeholders (e.g., employees and shareholders) will suffer financial consequences as a result

of that behavior (whistleblowing). In either case, the whistleblower may possess feelings of discomfort because of the conflict between his or her behavior (whistleblowing) and its undesirable, potential consequences (Smaili & Arroyo, 2019, p. 101).

To mitigate the feeling of discomfort of whistleblowers, organization leadership may create a climate that influences the success of whistle blower claims. Morales et al. (2014) contended that having a vivid and anonymous whistleblower hotline can deter fraud since the organizational climate and tone at the top can promote a particular organizational culture. McNeal (2016) outlined a few other best policies for a successful whistle blower policy. McNeal (2016) posited that one of the main features of a good whistle blower policy is enterprises having an open door policy. Employees would have the ability to freely speak about possible insidious acts against their organization. Employees should have the opportunity to freely and informally approach their manager and at a manager's discretion take it up the chain of command to determine the legitimacy of the claim of employees. McNeal (2016) continued that successful whistle blower policies will provided strict confidentiality to whistleblowers by protecting against retaliation, however, it does not protect the whistleblower from being subject to disciplinary actions for established personal malfeasance. RNPOs are no exception to fraud. Thus, having a robust whistle blower policy can certainly aide management and the organization in its plight to deter and detect fraud throughout the State of New Jersey.

Management Information System as a Deterrence Mechanism. It is impossible for managers, administrators, management, and employees to see everything at all times as it pertains to fraudulent activities of fraudsters. As indicated previously, fraudsters are complex and what triggers their behavior varies. However, management information technology can be a double edged sword. Segal (2016) pointed out that the explosion of computer-based resources opened the portal for a new kind of computer based fraud. Computer based technologies have left organizations in fear of what vulnerabilities may exist. However, in recent years organizations worldwide have incorporated management information systems to be their proverbial basketball sixth man in their attempt to thwart the attempts of would be schemers. Fraud detection software have help mitigate fraud in the business world (Segal, 2016). Segal identifies several types of software and information programs that have assisted management in enterprises worldwide. A technological technique used to assist in proper accounting governance is data mining (Segal, 2016; Sharma & Panigraphi, 2013). The use of data mining techniques enable administrators to automate the entire process of testing and scanning various reports for anomalies such as fraudulent payroll by accountant and administrators, fraudulent workers, and suppliers on a report (Sharma & Panigraphi, 2013). Segal (2016) identified five different information technology solutions that companies worldwide have incorporated into their businesses and organizations. Apart from the benefits mentioned earlier, Segal pointed out some the information technology solutions assist organizations identifying vulnerabilities probing for weaknesses. One software evaluates employee workload. Segal (2016) indicated that one of the information technology systems takes pre-emptive action if necessary to intercept and identify suspicious activities identifying new and emerging fraud patterns. Another information system detects anomalies visualization for multivariate and univariate outlier detections, using dynamic profiling and anomaly detection based on time series data (Segal, 2016). Segal (2016) acknowledged there are other non-fraud detection advantages, but provides assistance in other areas of management such as building analytic models that can be utilized for interactive data reporting, analysis, and visualization. Another information system technology that management of RNPOs can utilize is advanced email technologies. Segal (2016) continued that email is one of the leading ways that is primarily used in fictitious dealings.

Segal (2016) identified that Extensible Business Reporting Language (XBRL) is an information technological system that was developed to enable entities of financial reports to compare, read, and analyze between reports published in different languages and in different countries easily and efficiently and to enable in the long-run the publishing of financial reports in real time. Segal (2016) continued that XBRLs enable automated comparison and analysis of reports and easy comparison of financial and operational relations of companies throughout the world. XBRL is able to:

- Provide a database-like structure, using text files
- Define a collection of financial facts for a specific report, industry, and jurisdiction (taxonomy)
- Facilitate the data exchange between proprietary systems
- Promotes the re-use of data with far less effort.

Unfortunately, many RNPOs operate on thin margins and the cost of information technology to detect and deter fraud in their organizations in the State of New Jersey may be prohibitive.

Impact of Lack Deterrence Systems in RNPOs

RNPOs are not like some large for profit companies that have millions and sometimes billions of dollars in cash reserves on their balance sheet. Many of these entities are totally dependent on the mercies of donors and grants to make their payroll and carrying out their mission from month to month. If a grantor stops giving a grant, a RNPO could be out of business permanently within a matter of weeks. Because of the nature of RNPOs, obtaining loans and financing is much more difficult than a for profit enterprise. In many cases RNPOs do not have inventory because of the altruistic work. Also, the religious stigma and overtones, even issues with getting government funding because of "State versus church or religious organization," RNPOs find themselves totally dependent on people who share an affinity with the organization, thus reducing the pool of donors and entities that are willing to provide grants. So, fraud can have a devastating impact on RNPOs causing them to go out of business. However, there are other factors that determine if a RNPO totally collapses. One factor that Archambeault and Webber (2018) identified that may or may not cause a total ruin of an enterprise is age and size of the enterprise. There are several challenges associated with the age and size that determines the demise of a RNPO if fraud is discovered. Archambeault and Webber (2018) posited that younger entities have greater challenges their older counterparts may not have, such as lack of structure, lack of external legitimization, accountability problems, lack of reputation, liabilities with smallness, even the economies of scales affects whether an organization survives public relations impact of fraud in their organization. Another factor posited by Archambeault and Webber (2018) is the size of the fraud loss. Despite the age and size of an organization, larger fraud losses invariably have an impact on any organization.

A third variable that ultimately determines whether an enterprise recovers from fraud is the nature of the fraud (Archambeault & Webber, 2018). According to Archambeault and Webber (2018) there are two types of fraud classifications. Type one are occurrences where nonprofit enterprises victimize the public (e.g., improperly claiming government funds or filing false documents). Class two are situations where an employee or management within a nonprofit entity maltreated the organization (e.g., embezzlement or misappropriation of funds). The fourth reason occurs when a RNPO endures a fraudulent event depending on the organizational role of the fraudster. Archambeault and Webber (2018) found that the higher the level of the perpetrator in the organization, the more difficult it is for an entity to recover from an incident of fraud.

Themes and Perceptions

Religious not for profit organizations are no different than regular not for profit organizations and for-profit organizations when it comes to the potential of fraud, other than RNPOs embrace an overarching religious philosophical perspective that is integrated into the fabric of their organizations. One of the themes from the literature according to the results of Harris et al.'s (2017) study using a sample of 764 charities that reported asset diversion from 2008 to 2012, is if charitable entities had good governance it would have mitigated the likelihood of misappropriated funds. Similarly, Al-Halabi (2018) found in their study of Syrian banks that there was a positive relationship with trained leadership and the deterrence of people committing accounting fraud. The researcher believes that through the incorporation of proper leadership in RNPOs in New Jersey would-be-fraudsters, actions can be thwarted. Another theme that was identified in the literature in this study is internal control, and other fraud detection methods can provide accuracy in financial reporting, protect the misappropriation of funds, and aids with compliance; as with any other corporation protects organizations against financial abuses (Enofe & Amaria, 2011). Fraud deterrent measures such as proper training of staff how to detect behavioral and financial red flags, training on code of conduct and fraud and whistleblower policies that would encourage employees and volunteers to name a few can certainly be useful to administrators in denominational and non-denominational churches, and other religious organizations can curtail financial fraud (Enofe & Amaria, 2011; Wells, 2013). Another argument that was promulgated in the literature of this study is multifaceted reasons why fraud occurs in

RNPOs. One of the primary reasons cited by Shaharuddin and Sulaiman (2015) is the tremendous trust that RNPO's management places in their volunteers and employees. Shaharuddin and Sulaiman (2015) continued that leadership's lack of financial acumen and training contributes to the perfect atmosphere for financial fraud. Lastly, a high turnover of employees and volunteers can undoubtedly impact the failures of proper oversight of organization financial records.

Continuing in the thread of the human element of fraud in RNPOs and perhaps the most significant theme that the literature of this study focuses on is the psychological condition of fraudsters who commit fraud. Cressey (1953) identified that people commit fraud because of pressures such as sudden unexpected emergencies such as car repairs, drug abuse, greed, living beyond one's means, to name a few. The other thing that exists among fraudsters in these organizations is the perceived or actual opportunity (Roden et al., 2016). Finally, as part of Cressey FTT the study will show the people who commit fraud often will rationalize or justify their nefarious acts by making statements such as *everyone else does it.* Another statement made by perpetrators of fraud is *they do not pay us as volunteers so the theft is the least the organization can do for me.* The aforementioned are some of the themes in this study of RNPOs leadership ability to detect and deter fraud that may potentially show its hideous head in these well intentional entities in the State of New Jersey.

Summary of Literature Review

The literature review discussed and explained three primary constructs: (a) the behavioral and psychological component of why fraudster commit fraud; (b) a few types of governance structure that can thwart would be schemers; and (c) the COSO framework, including rules for ideal internal controls to detect and deter fraud that can happen in religious not for profit organizations in the state of New Jersey. Regarding the socio-psychological component, the literature explained the Fraud Triangle Theory pointing out that fraudsters may be motivated by various financial pressures, opportunity may exist to commit fraud, and finally fraudsters may possess the capacity to rationalize their wrong behavior. The review also discussed some contemporary theories such as the Diamond Fraud theory which added the element of capacity. Other theories included in the literature review and of why fraudsters commit fraud. This included the Fraud Scale theory which replaced Cressey's rationalization with a person of integrity arguing that people with high integrity may have opportunities and the financial stressor but will not commit fraud against their organization. The agency theory explained that because of egos and selfishness, schemers operate contrarily to what the principle agent implied and the explicit contract they originally had with the principle of the entity. The motivated reason theory which primarily applied to auditors of financial records shows that they sometimes are driven by good results and pleasing managers. The MICE theory, the socio-psychological theory, explained that money, ideology, coercion ego or entitlement are the basis of why some people commit fraudulent acts against RNPOS in the state of New Jersey.

The literature review explained that governance such as competency based, tone at the top, servant leadership, and spiritual intelligent leadership styles of governance may assist RNPOs in detecting and deterring fraud. The literature review also explained that having fraud detection techniques such as code of ethics and fraud training, red flags, whistle blowing policy, and management information system can aid enterprises in their effort to detect and deter fraud. The literature review explained what ideal deterrence systems are and what the reality is in some RNPOs. Finally, the literature pointed out the dependence of RNPOs on stakeholder's contributions and the impact that fraud can have on these altruistic organizations.

Section 2:

Introduction

This qualitative multi- case study explored the challenges of leaderships' ability to detect and deter fraud using internal controls in RNPOs in the State of New Jersey. The devastation of accounting fraud has ravaged several organizations, and the implications cannot be easily calculated. In contrast to for profit organizations, there is not much literature written on the topic fraud detection and prevention specific to religious not for profit organizations (Harris et al., 2017).

This study is intended to contribute to the research in the RNPO sector. The researcher mapped this multi case study research vis-à-vis the success of RNPO's administrator to detect and deter fraud in their organizations. The following sections will include: (i) purpose statement, (ii) role of the researcher, (iii) participants, research method and design, (iv) population and sampling, (v) data collection (techniques, collection technique, data organization techniques), (vi) data analysis technique, and (vii) reliability and validity and concluding with summary of the research methodology.

Purpose Statement

The purpose of this qualitative case study is to explore the problem of leaders of religious not-for-profit organizations (RNPOs) inability to identify and implement what are adequate internal accounting controls in their organizations throughout the State of New Jersey to deter various forms of accounting fraud. Religious Not for Profits organizations for centuries have provided valuable services to their local communities worldwide. RNPOs rely heavily on grants, voluntary gifts of donors, and inexpensive or free labor of volunteers. The fundamental aim of this study is to contribute to the body of literature that exists about leaders of RNPOs understanding of governance practices of their entities, the stewardship of their entities' assets and tools such as internal controls that are available to them thwarting would-be perpetrators of accounting fraud in their organizations (Pulido, 2018).

Role of the Researcher

One of the traits of a good researcher, according to Stake (2010), is he or she lays out an organized plan based on the research questions. Stake (2010) continued part of that plan is to obtain suitable aggregate and interpretive data. To satisfy this premise, the researcher collected data from participants such as RNPO's accountants, financial stewards, church leaders, organization administrators, board members, committee members, pastors, rabbis, and imam, or anyone in the organization that had fiscal oversight for this multi-case study. The researcher identified two sources of suitable participants. The first source was the State of New Jersey's Department of Consumer Affairs registry of charitable organizations in the State of New Jersey. The second source that the researcher utilized to obtain actors that desired to participate in the research was from a Christian college database of RNPOs that the researcher works as an adjunct instructor.

The researcher then created a list of email addresses and phone numbers in a Microsoft Excel spreadsheet of potential RNPOs that may want to participate in the interviewing process. The researcher then grouped the RNPOs that were available for an in-person interview and those that were unable to conduct face-to-face interviews the researcher employed the interview utilizing an online software program named Web Ex that allows users to communicate virtually via computer video cameras. To ensure the accuracy of face-to-face or over the phone information gathering, the researcher employed an electronic recorder and a writing pad to draft notes. After the interview, the researcher utilized a coding software named NVivo to assist in transcribing and coding data results into useful information in the analysis of research results.

Participants

In any qualitative study, gaining access to the 'right' participants is paramount to a successful research (Nakhid, 2015). As aforementioned, the State of New Jersey Department of Consumer Affairs provides the public with an archive of charitable organizations that operates in the state. This archive provides the researcher with a list of active RNPOs it can glean from of potential willing participants. To determine if the organization was active, the researcher matched the names against online yellow and white pages to determine if the entity was serving the public. The second group of organizations available to the researcher came from a database of RNPOs that the director of strategic alliance and outreach of a Christian college provided.

With the former group, the researcher determined that pointing out some of the pros and cons of detecting and deterring fraud in RNPOs may stimulate conversation and interest in the study. With the latter group, a personal introduction from the previously mentioned director of strategic alliances and outreach can establish a relationship with participants and potentially reduced the anxiety that may be associated with interviewing the leaders of these enterprises. The researcher found that besides face-to-face interviews, the Web Ex interviewing method reaped a couple of practical advantages such as broader reach, and the ability of pausing and stopping the interview (Smith et al., 2018).

Leaders of the selected RNPOs were reassured that the research followed all piloted ethical guidelines from Liberty University and was designed for protecting confidentiality and anonymity. In addition, all participants were given a non-disclosure and confidentiality agreement outlining the term of the study to reduce anxiety and increase participants' comfort. To bolster participants' confidence, the researcher explained once the online or face to face interview was completed, any organization's identifying information would be removed and identifying organization data deleted, so their information is kept private.

Research Method and Design

The research method and design of a study is an attempt by researchers to provide a roadmap of a study plan where data are collected, measured, and analyzed to test or create theories (Stake, 2010). The choice of electing the multi-case study qualitative method by the researcher is couched in the research questions and the purpose of the study. Moore et al. (2015) added that multi-case reviews look at unanticipated or complex casual pathway as in this study of RNPOs leaders' inability to identify and implement adequate internal accounting controls in their organizations to detect and deter accounting fraud in the State of New Jersey. This section will amplify the logic for selecting this method and design.

Discussion of Method

Contemporary researchers have three primary paradigms available to them quantitative, qualitative, and a combination of both— mix method. Moore et al. (2015) submitted that the data available and the research questions determine which mode researchers select. The overarching intent of qualitative studies is it aims to obtain an explanation and understanding of the larger picture or experience of participants (Stake, 2010). From another lens, qualitative methods intend to find and develop a holistic picture from a complex set of themes of the phenomena investigated, as with this study (Creswell, 2016). The qualitative study method fits this study because the research deals with some complex themes, such as why fraud is committed against altruistic entities and what internal control leaders have in place to thwart would-be fraudsters. A rudimentary viewpoint of qualitative research methods is a distinct inquiry process and inquiry that explores a human or a social problem typically answering how and what questions as with this study (Crabtree & Miller, 1999; Creswell, 2016; Silverman, 2000; Srivastava & Thomson, 2009). The research method was appropriate for this study because one of the questions that the researcher seeks to answer to the social problems of fraud in religious not for profits is what mechanisms or internal controls, if any, RNPOs have in place to prevent accounting fraud?

Another aspect of qualitative research methods is it is context-bound in that each participant embraces a subjective viewpoint of the topic. Still, patterns and theories can be explicated, and an understanding can be developed of a situation or phenomenon (Simon & Goes, 2013). Creswell and Poth (2016) postulated that qualitative research hinges heavily on the interpretations of participants, acquired through asking broad general questions, collecting data primarily from participants' words, describing and analyzing the participants written or recorded words for themes, and conducting inquiries in a subjective unbiased manner.

A less salient aspect of qualitative techniques is it allows researchers the ability to research a natural or organic setting employing multiple methods of data collection (Yin, 2014). This choice was appealing to the researcher because it allowed the researcher to meet with RNPOs financial administrators and leaders in their places of worship and business, perhaps reducing the anxiety of being in a controlled and less comfortable setting. The choice of qualitative method is grounded in the characteristics mentioned earlier of qualitative methodology and was integrated into this study enabling the research to add to the body of knowledge available to pundits, practitioners, and scholars alike.

Discussion of Design

As with research methods, researchers can also choose from a myriad of research designs. Creswell (2015) acknowledged 28 approaches that fall into five main categories; case study, ethnographic, grounded study, phenomenological, and narrative research design. Despite the researcher's choice of designs, all research designs provide a detailed outline or blueprint for fulfilling the research objectives for collecting, measuring, and analyzing the study's data (Cooper & Schindler, 2008). One qualitative method design available to researchers is a multiple case study. Yin (2014) borrows from Schramm's (1971) definition of a case study, which is he defines it as a tool that attempts to illuminate a decision or set of decisions indicating why they were taken, how they were implemented, and finally with what result (p. 15). Percy et al. (2015) and Creswell (2015) identified a case study as a qualitative approach in which the researcher reconnoiters a real-life, contemporary bounded system (a case) or multiple bound systems (cases) over time, through detailed, in-depth data collection involving multiple sources of information, and reports a case description and case themes or a study that differentiates one instance of the same phenomenon from another study (Bartlett & Vavrus, 2017). Percy et al. (2015) continued that case study methodology is continuously evolving and regularly reinterpreted however fundamentally comparative or multiple case studies are used as a tool for conflating information across time and space and occurs when a number of instance of the target are studied and then compared with one another as with this study. Delving deeper, Creswell (2015) and Alpi and Evans (2019) submitted that micro multi-case studies occur in a short-lived period, happen in a limited setting, and are relatively simple and straightforward. Alpi and Evans (2019) continued that a micro-level case describes an apparent problem of interest. Reporting is very brief and about specific points. The lack of complexity in the case description makes distinct the "lesson" that is inherent in the case. However, no definitive 'solution' is necessarily forthcoming, making the evidence useful for discussions.

The multi-case method was apt for this study because the investigator only sought to compare leaders of RNPOs viewpoint of internal controls and fraud in their organizations over a limited period. The theoretical replication bolsters the validity of the research, and readers may view the study as more compelling. The researcher selected the multi-case design because, unlike single case studies which focus on one case, the multi-case study allows the researcher to target multiple financial administrators' or leaders in RNPOs comparing their responses to determine if they share the same perspective of internal controls and its importance in detecting and deterring fraud. Yin (2014) submitted that case study research provides a robust basis for analysis and interpretation in the business environment because it is cradled in the natural environment of the phenomenon. Qualitative multiple case study method allows participants to answer open-ended questions, thereby allowing researchers to document variables that may go outside the hypothesis created in quantitative methods (Yin, 2014).

The study of leaders in RNPOs inability to identify and implement adequate internal accounting controls in their organizations to detect and deter accounting fraud in the State of New Jersey certainly possesses many of these theoretical complexities. Yin (2014) also argued that a multi-case study is a design tool utilized by researchers to contribute to the knowledge of the phenomenon of organizations, individuals, or groups. The uniqueness of this study certainly possesses characteristics in that religious organizations are not ordinarily studied to determine the causes of fraud or lack of internal controls. Finally, multiple case study was an appropriate choice for this study because as with the case of single-case design, the researcher does not want to put all its eggs into one basket.

Sample and Population

The fabric of the United States of America was woven with religious liberties and the latitude to freely exercise one's religious belief without fear. This first amendment right protects organizations and individuals. As such, there are large amounts of religious organizations throughout the United States; most of them are not for or non-profit (Colombo, 2017). Guidestar (2020) pointed out that there are over one hundred thousand religious nonprofit organizations in the United States. The state of New Jersey Department of Community Affairs (DCA), New Jersey's arm of government that tracks charitable organizations, acknowledges there are over 4000 charitable organizations registered in the State of New Jersey. Shorten and Moorley (2014) found "good sample selection and appropriate sample size strengthen a study, saving valuable time, money and resources" (para. 1). Completing a study of all RNPOs in the State of New Jersey would be cost prohibitive and extremely complex. Therefore, the researcher has opted to incorporate purposeful qualitative sampling techniques in the study. Creswell (2015) opined that in qualitative research, unlike quantitative research, which looks at a sample with the intent to generalize from the sample, the qualitative sample looks at a few individuals to provide an in-depth understanding of the phenomena studied. Creswell and Poth (2018) found there are three characteristics of purposeful sampling—the sample size studied, the sampling strategy, and the participants.

As indicated earlier, the sample size in qualitative studies is vital to the legitimacy of the study. Sample adequacy in qualitative inquiry is an essential consideration in assessments of the trustworthiness and quality in addition to the appraisals of validity and generalizability of the study (Vasileiou et al., 2018). Shorten and Moorley (2014) continued that in qualitative studies, that sample can be as small as one and end at saturation point. Vasileiou et al. (2018) and Baker and Edwards (2012) acknowledged that some pundits of qualitative research contended that there is no clear-cut answer to the question of 'what is the ideal sample size,' but rather it is based on factors relating to epistemological, methodological and practical issues. Nonetheless, most research authorities agree the gold standard of qualitative inquiries for an ideal sample size happens at saturation point or at the point when obtaining additional data through interviews yield no new insights, no additional discoveries 'no new data,' 'no new themes,' and 'no new codes' (Creswell & Poth, 2018; Vasileiou et al., 2018). Yin (2014) postulated that 6 to 10 is an adequate sample size for multiple case studies. Thus, the researcher is applying this technique to the study of leaders' inability to detect and deter fraud using internal control in RNPOs in the state of New Jersey.

The sampling strategy in this study, as aforementioned, involves the researcher using a multiple prong approach where the researcher visits participants' on-site at their various places of worship and operations and the use of Web Ex interactive conferencing. The researcher intends to interview financial administrators, rabbi, imams, pastors, or any organizational leader of RNPOs that have an intimate knowledge of the accounting strategy of their organizations because it is highly likely these people would know the inner working of the financial system of their organization. Due to the researcher's affiliations to an evangelical school in the State of New Jersey, he used this purposeful sampling. The researcher does not know any of the participants per se, which lends to the reliability and validity of the sample. Using the purposeful sampling technique, the researcher would be able to obtain information-rich data from participants of each interview identified earlier.

Data Collection

Qualitative researchers have a plethora of methods from interviews, to focus groups to collect data. Despite the method chosen with any qualitative or quantitative study the collection of high quality data along with the extraction and exploration of textual data to describe and explain the phenomena being researched is of paramount importance when conducting an investigation

(Gelling, 2015). This section of the study chronicles the instrument, collection technique, the data organization, and data analysis techniques used.

Instruments

The instrument or instruments also play a critical role in the collection of data in research. Creswell (2015) posited that a solid research plan requires a thorough discussion about the research instrument—its development, its scales, its items, and reports of reliability and validity. Unlike quantitative investigations, with qualitative research, the researcher is the instrument of the study. Creswell (2015) continued that qualitative researchers act as the instrument, collecting data, observing behavior, interviewing participants, and examining documents. Qualitative researchers may use practices such as writing pads and audio tape recorders for collecting data, but ultimately, the researchers are the ones who gather the information. For this study, the research opted to conduct face to face and Web-Ex, Zoom, or Facebook interviews to get a better understanding if financial administrators of RNPOs comprehend what fraud is and if they understand that one of the tools available to them to detect and deter fraud is accounting internal controls. However, a rapport must be established with participants before the researcher can obtain any information.

Pezalla et al. (2012) argued that interviewers should conduct a semi-structured interview where the researcher facilitates the conversation to create a conversational safe and comfortable space where the participants are willing to share information-rich data after establishing a connection with interviewers. Pezalla et al. (2012) asserted participants might experience a feeling of interpersonal connection that is necessary between qualitative interviewer and interviewee perhaps establishing a conversation space and mutual understanding. After a rapport is established, one tool available to researchers in their quest to obtain gainful insight in the interviewing process is an interview guide. Pedersen et al. (2016) described an interview guide as an instrument that assists the interviewer's posing questions relevant to the topic of interest and supports consistency in each case interview and aids with linking the research questions, research problem, and past relevant literature. The researcher employed an interview guide to stay focused on the topic and thoroughly examine the participant's knowledge of the subject of fraud and accounting internal controls.

In this study, the primary question the researcher asked was what internal accounting controls, if any, your religious not for profit organization has in place to prevent accounting fraud? The second core question to the leader is what is your perspective of the minimal internal controls to deter accounting fraud in your organization? The researcher provided a more comprehensive list of 25 research questions outlined in Appendix A. The researcher developed the interview guide using the problem statement as its premise, which discusses leaders of RNPOs and small business owners' inability to identify and implement what are adequate internal accounting controls in their organizations to deter accounting fraud. The introductory statement of the interview guide acknowledged the importance of RNPOs and their role in society. The introduction continues that fraud could be catastrophic for any RNPO because religious organizations are often held to a higher standard than other NPOs. The closing statement of the interview guide will indicate to leaders that their financial vigilance is critical to preventing fraud despite hiring high character personnel and volunteers in their organization.

Data Collection Technique

Unlike structured interviews using an interview guide where the interviewer controls what the questions would look like. In multi-case studies, the investigator is subject to the interviewees' schedule, and availability. Sometimes the interviewee may digress from the line of questioning posed by interviewer (Yin, 2014). Thus, the researcher must design an interview protocol to deal with deviations and other issues that may arise during the interviews. Stake (2010) purported that creating a well-developed protocol can save researchers time and bolster meaningfulness to the research. Nonetheless, Percy et al. (2015) asserted there are at least 15 types of data sources that a researcher can employ. Percy et al. (2015) continued that multi-cases studies data collection should use multiple data sources. Still, archetypical the majority of the raw data are obtained via in-depth conversations between the interviewer and the participants. For this study, the researcher has opted to use face to face and Web-Ex virtual interviews, participant observations, the recording of field notes in a diary, and conversation recording in an audio recorder.

With face to face and Web-Ex interviews, the researcher contacted and arranged with leaders of each RNPOs a time, date, and place that was most convenient for them. The researcher indicated in the letter or email to each interviewer that the interview would take between one to one and a half hours of their time. Each interview was audio-recorded to ensure that any information was not captured in the interviewer's diary was captured on a digital recorder. The interviewer immediately transcribed the data on paper shortly after the interview to ensure none of the information was lost.

Next, the interviewer requested pertinent documentation that would aid in the study from the RNPO's leaders with the assurance all documents would be eventually destroyed upon completion of the study. Copies of the documents were done on-site at the RNPOs using a copying machine. If the organization did not have a copier available, the researcher requested that the document be emailed to the interviewer's email address in a secured fashion. The email was sent using the secured feature of Microsoft Word, which locked the document, and a password had to be entered to unlock the document by the receiver.

To ensure the accuracy of the data, the interviewer incorporated member checking technique. Stake (2010) acknowledged that member checking, or the process of discussing the recorded draft with participants to determine if the data collected needs correction and any additional comments are necessary to ensure accuracy. This procedure should ensure the data collected were accurate and the interviewer clearly articulated the questions.

Data Organization Technique

Sherif (2018) found that systematic data organization and archiving is an ongoing process co-occurring with data collection (para. 18). The researcher organized and saved field notes or the Microsoft Word copy of each interview guide in electronic folders on the laptop immediately after each interview. Each folder was labeled with the organizations' name, and the person who was interviewed. If the organization leader interviewed did not want to disclose the name of the organization or their name, a pseudonym was used to mask their identity. As a back up to the field notes, the interviewer backed up all data that were on the desktop to an external flash drive. In the same folder, the researcher also transferred the audio recording from his Apple I-phone or I-Pad to the corresponding file where the written interview guide was saved, ensuring harmony with the written and digital copy of the interview. Once member checking was completed for accuracy and completeness. The interviewer uploaded the data into NVivo 12, a software program that aids the researcher with coding to find related themes.

Data Analysis

The collection of raw data is useless and meaningless to readers unless it provides insight into the study. To give qualitative studies significance, researchers rely heavily on robust data analysis. Bogdan and Biklen (1999, as cited in Simon & Goes, 2013) viewed data analysis as the process of breaking and organizing data into manageable parts for the purpose of synthesizing it, examining for patterns, and discovering what is essential and what is to be learned to communicate to the researcher's desired audience. There are a few techniques used to analyze data, but according to Simon and Goes (2013), there is no consensus on what is the best method for multi-case studies. However, Percy et al. (2015) pointed out that Stake (2010) and Creswell (2015) agreed there are a few necessary steps associated with all data analysis.

The first step was the descriptive step where the investigator created a detailed description of the case as a whole, its settings and contexts providing a detail, clarity, and creating a textured, rich picture of the case and its settings. The second step, direct interpretation, pulled the data apart in each case and reconstructed it in a more meaningful way so the researcher could draw meaning from the described data. The third step, categorical aggregation, was where the researcher sought to collect meaning rich occurrences from the data, putting it into specific categories of significance. The fourth step was where investigators identified common themes, statements, and patterns relying on verbatim passages and direct quotes. Then the investigator developed thematic analysis across cases as well as interpretations of the integrated meaning of all the evidence in the study. Yin (2014) found that with case studies, computer-assisted tools such as HyperRESEARCH or NVivo are invaluable in coding and extracting meaningful patterns from field notes. Finally, the interpretative stage was where the researcher developed naturalized generalizations from the data as a whole and reported on the lessons learned from the study.

Embracing the steps mentioned earlier as the basis of this study data analysis, the researcher re-read the field notes which were collected using the interview guide of each participant thoroughly for clarity. Yin (2014) stated it 'played' with the data searching for arrays creating a detailed description of each case as a whole.

After playing with the data, the researcher juxtaposed interviews, pattern matching against the theoretical framework of the research in an attempt to determine if there were commonalities from each meeting. After finding commonalities, the interviewer then synthesized the data. The categories the researcher used to summarize the data were leadership competencies of governance, leadership understanding of fraud, and leadership understanding of internal controls. To accelerate the process, the researcher utilized NVivo 12 to assist in the thematic coding process. Finally, the use of the NVivo 12 software tool in the coding process enabled the interviewer to interpret, create naturalized generalizations from the data as a whole, and report on the lessons learned from the study of leaders in RNPOs' ability to deter and detect fraud in their institutions.

Reliability and Validity

Both qualitative and quantitative investigators desired to establish the credibility of their arguments promulgated in their studies. Two tools researchers utilized and were almost always paired together in the explanation building of research were reliability and validity.

Reliability

Conceptually there are several sub-categories of reliability and validity; however, cradling Simon and Goes (2013) as does Hayashi Abib and Hoppen's (2019) classification of reliability, reliability is the evaluation of the accuracy, repeatability, and consistency of results over a period. Unlike quantitative studies where reliability is concerned with the replication of the results, qualitative reliability is where the researcher is consistent across different projects (Creswell, 2015; Simon & Goes, 2013). Simon and Goes (2013) and Yin (2014) continued that reliability in qualitative studies' objective is to mitigate the influence of bias or influences of the researcher conducting the research. Yin (2014) and Thyer (2009) posited that skilled interviewers adopt the following in their investigation to increase dependability or reliability.

Adopting a questioning process is a method that requires participants to provide an explicit perspective that guards against socially desirable responses (Thyer, 2009). In the study of RNPOs leaders' inability to detect and deter fraud in their organizations, the researcher developed a 25-question focus interview guide to mitigate socially desirable responses. The questions were designed to probe and determine the RNPO leader's financial competence and their knowledge of internal controls.

The second suggestion that Thyer (2009) proposed to strengthen a study's reliability by creating a robust recording procedure of field notes. Thyer (2009) offered that researchers can utilize all four field notes: (a) a condensed or verbatim account; (b) an expanded account of the interview; (c) a fieldwork journal that contains a more reflective experience such as emotions, ideas, mistakes, and concerns; and (d) a running record of the analysis and interpretation while in the field. In this study, the researcher planned to adopt a few of the suggestions above. The interviewer used an audio recorder along with a journal to record the interview verbatim. In addition, the interviewer kept a log of each participant's reaction and emotions during each interview.

The third technique, the use of computer software aids, strengthened the reliability of the research (Thyer, 2009; Yin, 2014). Many programs, such as NVivo 12, enabled researchers to manage data using color schemes, word processing programs, folders, and tools that aid in developing themes. A final recommendation purported by Thyer (2009) was cross-checking using software tools. Tyher (2009) suggested that cross-checking coding improves reliability, which the researcher incorporated in to this study. Through the use of this tool and other tools, researchers are able to build confidence in readers of the reliability of the data submitted in their arguments.

Validity

There is no validity without establishing reliability. A robust research design is only as good as its weakest link. Researchers seek to establish that their studies are credible, congruent, relevant to audiences, and the intended reality obtained from the perspectives of those who provided data (Creswell & Poth, 2018; Daniel, 2018). Validity is the degree or extent that the instrument or the researcher measures what they intended to measure (Simon & Goes, 2015). Creswell and Poth (2018) made eight suggestions to accomplish the feat of credibility, which they further narrowed into two constructs—from the researchers and participants' lens. The investigator only utilized a few.

The overarching strategy used is triangulation. Stake (2010) claimed that a qualitative study is done well when it is properly triangulated, or the researcher got the meaning straight by looking at multiple sources of data. Creswell (2015) argued that through cross-examining of different data sources, researchers could build a coherent justification for themes. The cross-examination of several data sources also enables investigators to establish vivid perspectives from participants. Triangulation includes member checks, researcher's field notes, structured, focus, and open-ended interviews, and archival records (Yin, 2014). The process mentioned earlier was viewed as adding validity to the study. In the case of this study, the researcher looked at the interview guides as a form of focused interviews of all the participants, and as a means of bolstering the credibility of the study.

The second aspect of triangulation used in validating a study is member checking. Member checking is the process where researchers give back the participants or interviewees the information gathered, asking for correction and comments (Stake, 2010; Zulkipli & Baba, 2018). Member checking is a way for researchers to obtain accuracy and to determine if the data obtained may potentially have insensitive language and information (Stake, 2010). In this study, the research intended to double-check the data with leaders of RNPOs after the interviews were transcribed to validate the information was accurate and resembled what the participants intended during the interview.

Zulkipli and Baba (2018) promulgated that a third strategy in authenticating a qualitative multi-case study is “rich, thick descriptions or high quantity of information that can help in conceptualizing process and interpret the findings” (p. 55). Creswell and Poth (2018) asserted that a full description occurs when a case provides sufficient interconnected detail utilizing strong action verbs and quotes. Finally, Fusch and Ness (2015) purported “that failure to reach data saturation has an impact on the quality of the research conducted and hampers content validity” (p. 1408). It is a high probability if no new data and no new themes result from interviews (Fusch & Ness, 2015). It is highly likely that an interviewer has reached the data saturation point. So in sum, researchers could adopt the measures mentioned above to diminish researcher bias and bolster credibility to their research in the eyes of their readers (Creswell, 2016).

Transition and Summary

Though a soft science, multi-case qualitative studies marries the conceptual with practical application. The previous section of this study delineated and described in detail how the researcher planned to practically accomplish an in-depth understanding of RNPOs leaders’ inability to identify and implement adequate internal accounting controls in their organizations to detect and deter accounting fraud in the State of New Jersey. The previous section detailed the role of the researcher, the study's participants, the research method and design, sample and population, data collection and analysis, and the reliability and validity of the study. Along with the aforementioned, the previous section indicated where geographically the investigation took place.

The final section of this study chronicles how this scientific study fuses the conceptual with the practical detailing the researcher's research questions and accompanying fieldwork to support the conceptual framework. Besides the findings of the fieldwork, this study provides patterns and themes found from the field. Also included are the application, recommendations, and best practices for RNPOs practitioners' for protecting their institutions' assets and resources. Finally, the last section provide the researcher's summarized results and significant points for scholars, pundits, and practitioners to glean from for future studies.

Section 3:

Application to Professional Practice and Implications for Change

Overview of the Study

The purpose of this multi case qualitative study of the inability of leaders of RNPOs in the State of New Jersey to identify and implement adequate accounting internal controls to detect and deter accounting fraud was to add to the growing body of limited literature that exist about the subject of fraud, specifically in religious not for profit enterprises. There is a lack of pragmatic data and there was no established stream of literature addressing the long-term consequence of fraud on the existence of nonprofit organizations, especially religious and quasi-religious not for profit organizations (Archambeault & Webber, 2018). The study identified that fraud does not discriminate what business model it impacts. Invariably, most religious and quasi-religious entities exist to reduce the socio-economic plights of human. This study discusses that even these entities are not exempt from the blight of fraud. This section of the study focused on three primary areas: the process of fact finding, the results of the finding, and the assessment of results.

Anticipated Themes/Perceptions

Based on the literature review, the researcher determined there is very little difference between traditional not for profits and RNPOs as it pertains to the potential of fraud. The only difference is the religious philosophical perspective integrated into the fabric of their organizations. One of the anticipated themes was trained leaders and staff, which most likely would mitigate the likelihood of misappropriated funds. Similarly, Al-Halabi (2018) found in the study of Syrian banks there was a positive relationship with trained leadership and the deterrence of people committing accounting fraud. Shaharuddin and Sulaiman (2015) continued that leadership's lack of financial acumen and training positively contributes to the perfect atmosphere for financial fraud. The researcher believes through the incorporation of proper training for leadership and staff in RNPOs in New Jersey, fraudster's actions can be thwarted.

Another theme identified in the literature in this study was internal control. Other fraud detection methods can provide accuracy in financial reporting, protect the misappropriation of funds, and aids with compliance as with any other mechanisms against financial abuses (Enofe & Amaria, 2011). Fraud deterrent measures, including: (a) proper training of staff; (b) how to detect behavioral and financial red flags; and (c) training on code of conduct, fraud, and whistleblower policies that would encourage employees and volunteers, can certainly be useful to administrators in denominational and non-denominational churches, and other religious organizations can curtail financial fraud (Enofe & Amaria, 2011; Wells, 2013). Another argument promulgated in the literature of this study was multifaceted reasons why fraud occurs in RNPOs. A final theme or anticipated theme or perception was that fraud can occur in RNPOs. One of the primary reasons for fraud is the tremendous trust that RNPO's management places in their volunteers and employees (Shaharuddin & Sulaiman, 2015). Many leaders are not aware that fraud can occur in RNPOs.

Presentation of the Findings

The fact-finding process began with the researcher using an assorted variety of recruitment methods of finding 11 RNPO leaders. Initially, the researcher contacted 13 RNPO leaders, but only 10 were interested in conducting an interview. The saturation point could occur at 10 participants (Yin, 2014). Some referrals came from a partial Christian college database that the researcher works for part-time. Others came from going through a list of religious non-profits on the State of New Jersey Department of Community Affairs' website.

Finally, some referrals emanated from a member of a local church the researcher attends. After contacting each leader via telephone, electronic mail, and Facebook, the researcher scheduled a convenient time and date for both parties to conduct a Zoom video-conferencing interview. Because of the COVID-19 pandemic and the suitability of recording the meetings via a feature of the Zoom video conferencing application, the researcher concluded that it was prudent only to conduct Zoom interviews. After contacting interviewees and setting up the agreed-upon time and date, the researcher emailed a copy of the Institutional Review Board (IRB) approved consent form for interviewees to sign and return via email. The interviewer completed 10 interviews over four weeks. The saturation point occurred at the ninth interview, but the researcher did an additional interview to ensure there was no further information missed. The researcher employed note taking, the use of Zoom recording feature, the initial participants' interviews, and the member checking to triangulate the information gathered during interviews determining accuracy of the data.

General Background of RNPOs

The results of the findings showed a rich, diverse collection of RNPOs. There were three churches—one Baptist, one non-denominational, and a charismatic Pentecostal church. There was a Christian health care center that provided geriatric care and mental health services employing over 700 employees. One was a church missionary that supports and provides prostitutes with housing, education, and various services to help them find different careers. This missionary also funds schools and gives food to the poor in Africa, South America, Central America, and the Caribbean. There was a former deaconry that finds its genesis training deacons for a variety of churches, but now offers a rental retreat facility for Christian ministries and provides daycare and pre-kindergarten services. Another organization provides music lessons to both urban and suburban students at a minimal cost. Finally, one organization operates as a cancer support program for women who are battling cancer. The RNPOs range from one employee to 729. All the RNPOs were in the central and northern part of the State of New Jersey, perhaps because over 70% of the state's population lives in these two parts of New Jersey (NJ, 2019). Below is a summary of the leaders interviewed' biographic information, the size of the entity's budgets, and staff.

Table 3

Demographics of Participants and Size of Organization

Participants	Age Range	Gender	Years of Experience	Educational Level	Organizations Annual Budget	Organizations Staff size
1	30 – 39	Male	3.5	Master	$150,000	5 -12 volunteers
2	50-59	Female	4	Some college	$20,000	4 volunteers
3	60+	Male	3.5	Master	$2.75 million	75-80 paid and volunteers
4	30-39	Female	4	Master	$18,400	15 volunteers
5	40-49	Female	12	Master	$16,000	1 stipend
6	40-49	Male	1	Some college	$500,000	1 paid
7	50-59	Male	30	Master	$80 million	729 paid
8	30-39	Male	5	Bachelors	$265,000	5 paid; volunteers vary
9	60+	Female	20	Masters	$7 to $10,000	6-8 volunteers
10	60+	Female	5	PhD	$25,000	PhD

The researcher gathered the data outlined in this section and the data highlighted above using an interview guide (See Appendix A). An interview guide is an instrument that assists the interviewer's posing relevant questions of interest and supports consistency in each case interview and aids with linking the research questions, research problem, and past relevant literature (Pedersen et al., 2016). The researcher initially created a 28-question guide that eventually was reduced to 25 questions. The justification for reducing the interview guide to 25 questions was three of the questions were redundant. Nevertheless, the researcher's quest at this juncture of the study was primarily couched in obtaining data through two fundamental research questions.

Question 1: Is there a relationship between leadership competence, perception, leadership style, and fraud detection? The second question was what mechanisms or internal accounting controls, religious not-for-profit organizations, have to prevent accounting fraud. The first question, along with Questions 3, 7, 9, 10, 13, 15, 17, 21, and 23 in the interview guide, examined leaders' formal and informal education, professional training, and occupational skills that empowered them to detect and deter fraud in their organizations. The second question's primary purpose along with items 11, 12, 14, 16, 17, 18, 19, 20, and 21 of the interview guide was designed to determine if leaders of RNPOs understood what internal accounting controls were and them in place in their organization to protect their financial resources.

Research Question 1

In this study, the researcher summarized the universal background information about each RNPO leader. The interviewer did this for two reasons. First, the researcher did it to determine if there is a correlation between the leaders' backgrounds, preparing them in full, or in part to detect fraud in their enterprises. Second, the interviewer did it to create pattern matching between leaders. Yin (2014) purported that in multiple case studies to determine if there are similarities and unique interpretations, single intensive interviews are necessary to create a comparative structure.

The researcher's design of the tables and information in this section created pattern matching between leaders looking at similarities and themes (Yin, 2014). The basic information about the leader's background included the gender of each participant, age, formal education, type of leadership role in the RNPO, the period in that leadership role, and whether paid or volunteer.

Gender and Age

The rudimentary information revealed that there were precisely 50% of males and females (see table below). Another variable this study considered was the age of interviewees. To reduce the anxiety and protect participants' anonymity, the researcher collected age ranges versus the exact age, even though four of the participants provided their precise age. As shown earlier, Pezalla et al. (2012) contended that interviewers should facilitate the interview to create a conversational safe and comfortable space where the participants are willing to share information-rich data after establishing a connection with interviewers.

The researcher used the following age groups in the research study: (30-39), (40-49), (50-59), and 60+. The breakdown of participants in the research study comprised the following:

- 3 RNPO leaders (30.0%) – 30-39 age range
- 2 RNPO leaders (20.0%) – 40-49 age range
- 2 RNPO leaders (20.0%) – 50-59 age range
- 3 RNPO leaders (30.0%) – 60+ age range

The research finding showed the age range was almost evenly distributed. After examining the two variables of gender and age with respect to leaders in this research study, the researcher concluded that the findings did not shed any light on leaders' ability to detect and deter fraud in their organizations. Reflecting on the research question, there was no conclusive patterns to decide if age or gender made a difference in the deterrence and detection of fraud in RNPOs.

Formal Higher Education

The researcher then gathered data about the RNPOs leaders' formal, higher educational accomplishments. Below highlights the higher educational achievement for the leaders:

- 1 RNPO leader – (20.0%) Doctorate
- 6 RNPO leaders - (60.0%) Master
- 1 RNPO leader - (10.0%) Bachelor
- 2 RNPO leaders - (20.0%) Some College

The researcher looked at the higher educational level of RNPOs leaders to determine if there was any relationship between the leaders' education and their ability to comprehend accounting and financial information. Education conveys fresh, valuable skill sets, and knowledge in the workplace, assisting employees with the underlying ability to perform their jobs efficiently and knowledgeably (Toner & Woolley, 2016; Wolfe & Hermanson, 2004). Harris et al. (2017) pointed out that not-for-profit leaders are amateurs in governance positions in the stewardship of nonprofit organizations (NPO). Further, Steimel (2018) purported that often volunteers obtain little job training and many times are less credentialed.

The data in this study contradict these studies because at least 80% of employees, both volunteer and paid, had a bachelor's degree or higher. Besides, this study contradicts some previous findings in that 3 or 30% of the RNPOs leaders had a bachelor's or master's degree in business administration and were in their role an average of nine years. However, the researcher could not find any concrete evidence to support formal higher education by itself as a determinant of whether a leader understood internal accounting controls in the detection and deterrence of fraud. The results support one previous research that the nonprofit sector has progressed from the novices and volunteer staffing model to a more highly formalized staffing structure of subject matter experts, professional managers, and cost accountants (Feng et al., 2019; Hwang & Powell, 2009).

Accounting Education or Experience

Besides the formal higher education, the researcher delved deeper to determine if the leaders of the RNPOs had specific accounting education and experience that contributed to their ability to identify and deter fraud. Hughes et al. (2008) identified the leadership competency model as abilities, skills, knowledge, and other attributes that are relevant for a leader's success in a particular job, or as identified in this study, religious leaders' ability to successfully deter accounting fraud. Research Question 1 asked what competencies, accounting education, and accounting experience do you possess? Three or 30% of respondents said they had no accounting education and accounting experience as the organization's administrator in understanding internal financial controls. Two or 20% of interviewees had some accounting knowledge, but relied heavily on someone else to oversee the internal accounting controls. One or 10% of the respondents understood internal controls from a functional responsibility; she understood that excellent accounting practices require two people to sign checks and others to deposit funds, thus creating a separation of duties and responsibilities. However, that leader had no formal accounting training. Two or 20% were former financial administrators or a chief financial officer of organizations with a thorough understanding of internal accounting controls. One or 10% of RNPO leaders only had one college accounting class, and one or 10% received on-the-job experience in their understanding of internal controls.

Often, volunteers obtain little job training and many times are less credentialed (Steimel, 2018). This study contradicts the previous finding in that 30% of the participants had master's degrees coupled with experience as financial administrators and a CPA, making them capable academically and occupationally able to detect and deter fraud in their enterprises. Another part of Question 1 in the interview guide asked participants if they had any financial or accounting certification, such as Certified Public Accountant or Certified Financial Planner designation. Only one interviewee held a CPA designation.

Participant 7 stated, "He believes that being trained as a CPA and sitting on audit committees has empowered him to deal properly with the detection and deterrence of fraud in his organizations." Whereas Participant 10 had a Ph.D. and an MBA, she stated that even though she earned an MBA, which included some accounting education, she did not have any internal controls to detect or deter fraud. She continued that after the interview, she saw the importance of having them in place. Participant 8, who has a bachelor's degree, stated he does not believe in being a jack-of-all-trades and master of none. He went on to state 'he believes in hiring people who are content experts in their area.' He continued that he has pastored three churches, and the first thing he looks at when he starts his tenure at a new church is to look at the books or financial statements. He has used a reputable CPA for several years, and he has used them to complete a forensic look at the financial statements of each church he has pastored.

Often, volunteers obtain little job training and many times are less credentialed (Steimel, 2018). Gratton (2018) found that employees and volunteers at non-profits often lack the fundamental human resources skills and experience their for-profit equivalents possess. This study contradicts some of the traditional viewpoints in that RNPOs. Leaders interviewed showed that 80% of leaders had at least a bachelor's degree, and 20% of the leaders had significant experience as a CFO and another as a financial administrator. The findings show that participants' perspectives were the driver of the importance of internal accounting controls (Ventura & Daniel,

2010). This study refutes some previous studies because at least 20% had significant accounting experience and understanding of how to detect and deter fraud in their organizations. In addition, 30% had at least some accounting training or accounting experience in understanding accounting practices.

Volunteerism Versus Paid Employment

Another area of interest to the researcher in the fact-finding process in answering Research Question 1 was whether the interviewees were paid or were volunteers inside and/or outside of their organization. Questions 3 and 4 of the interview guide produced the following results of participants' work experience inside and outside of their entities:

Table 4

Responses to Questions 3 and 4

	Position outside RNPO	Position in RNPO
Participant 1	Partnership coordinator	Director
Participant 2	Part time home care	Administrator
Participant 3	None	Director
Participant 4	Teacher	Director
Participant 5	Self-employed music teacher	Director
Participant 6	None	Director
Participant 7	None	CEO
Participant 8	None	Pastor
Participant 9	Childcare center director	Director
Participant 10	Professor	Pastor

Fifty percent or five of the 10 participants were partially or fully paid employees of their organization, and the other five or 50% were volunteers. Forty percent of the interviewees were both founders and volunteers of their organizations. Only one volunteer or 10% of the participants was not the founder of their organization or had a full-time position in their RNPOs. Erasmu and

Morey (2016) noted that faith-based nonprofit organizations usually have a higher number of volunteers relative to other forms of not profit organization. The finding in this study showed it all depended on the organization's staff and budget size. The results show the larger organizations paid their leaders. Larger organizations are more likely to have greater capacity to implement strategies that ensure access to vital resources such as critical staffing for survival and growth of the organization (Davis & Cobb, 2009; Del Mar et al., 2016). Perhaps because these entities received more income and had more staff, they had much more to preserve. The findings of this study indicate that RNPOs who had paid leaders in turn had better internal controls in place.

Professional and Non-Professional Experience

The researcher asked RNPO leaders how has their professional or non-professional experience equipped them to detect potential fraud, mismanagement, misappropriation, or abuse in their religious entities? Prakash and Kumar (2016) found in their research that meaningful learning experiences do happen outside of the formal education institutions. Some learning happens in families, workplaces, and other organizations or institutional settings. All participants said they believe either their professional or non-professional experience had equipped them to detect fraud. Some skills are not developed in a formal setting, but some skills are developed on the job. Informal learning in many occasions is said to be more effective for learning job-related skills and competencies than traditional education (Eraut, 2004; Schürmann & Beausaert, 2016).

The interviewees provided the following about their various perceptions. Participant 4 stated she did not have any professional experience deterring or detecting fraud, but her non-professional experience through lived cultural experiences has aided her in detecting fraud. She also said all the funds received in her organization go through her, and recipients of the monies sent overseas need to provide receipts for any expenditures. Participant 7 posited his professional experience working for a major accounting firm for seven years and then as the chief financial officer for four years and the chief executive officer for another 26 years had aided him in detecting and deterring fraud in his organization. Participant 1 expressed that his professional and non-professional experience of creating hard copies and digital copies of all financial and accounting transactions has equipped him to deter financial abuse in his organization. One-hundred percent (100%) of the RNPOs leaders perceived their professional and non-professional experience in and outside of their organization had enabled them to detect and deter fraud in their entities.

Financial Decisions

Next, the researcher used Questions 5, 6, and 10 to establish if RNPOs leaders have made financial decisions on behalf of their organization and how long they have done so. These questions were asked to find out if the leaders selected were involved in making fiscal determinations on behalf of their entities. Ninety percent (90%) of leaders said they provided financial management support for their organizations. Only Participant 9 stated that someone else is entrusted with financial management support on behalf of the organization. Seventy percent (70%) or 7 of 10 of the leaders have made financial decisions for their organizations between 1 year and 5 years, and the additional 30% of leaders have made financial decisions for 12, 20, and 30 years, respectively.

Forty percent (40%) of interviewees make all their enterprises' financial decisions. Participant 3 expressed his home office makes most of the financial decisions. He said he makes some local financial decisions. Participant 5 stated she is involved in decisions pertaining to the expansion of the organization. I also have to approve and ask the treasurer to accept it. They include multiple board members in counting cash. Overall, 90% of RNPO leaders make financial decisions either partially or totally on behalf of their entity. This question was asked to ascertain the degree of financial involvement of leaders in their organizations' financial decision-making.

Fiduciary Responsibility

When asked Question 9 of the interview guide, 'Who do you believe has the fiduciary responsibility and oversight for protecting the organization's resources,' 100% of all respondents indicated the board of directors, and/or the pastor, and/or director, and/or administrators have the fiduciary oversight of the organization's resources. The researcher geared the question to determine the administrators' perspective concerning who was responsible for the fiduciary responsibly for protecting the organization's resources.

Rae et al. (2017) and Treadway Commission Report COSO (2017) noted the reliability of financial reports along with all other components of internal control hinges on the 'tone at the top' of an organization. Warren et al. (2015) opined that the tone at top theory is broadly accepted as one of the primary predictors of ethical behavior in organizations. Maboya and McKay (2019) pointed out that one item on the leadership minds of the not-for-profit organizations is having the skills and capacity to adequately managing the organization's finances and board oversight. The unanimous RNPOs perspective validates prior research that leaderships are profoundly concerned about protecting their organization's resources.

Additional Training

To better understand Research Question 1, the researcher asked Question 13 of the interview guide, 'What additional training is required for you to strengthen your financial competencies to adequately safeguard the organization's resources? Ninety percent (90%) or 9 of the interviewees said they needed some training. Participant 9 stated she believes she needed training because things are continually changing. Participant 5 stated given who her treasurer is, she does not believe she needs any training. She went on to assert her treasurer is an accounting guru. Participant 7 said one of the things he was most concerned about was cybersecurity. He said the use of technology had created some unintended consequences that he is worried about, and getting trained in those areas is what he would like.

Thomson et al. (2016) acknowledged that respondents of a one-year leadership training expressed that the ongoing training had 'very much' improved their ability to understand the results and they were able to complete an analysis. Overwhelmingly, leaders believe there was need to gain additional training because of the changing environment and their lack of adequate understanding of fraud in their organizations.

Research Question 2

Apart from obtaining an understanding of leadership competence, leadership style and fraud detection, the researcher was curious to find out what mechanisms or internal controls, religious not for profits organizations had in place to prevent accounting fraud. The interview guide questions in this section were designed to extract the 10 RNPOs leaders' perspective of what tools they had in place to deal with fraud.

Measures or Activities in Place to Deal With Fraud

The researcher explicitly tailored Question 11 of the interview guide to find out what activities and internal controls, if any, the leader's organization had in place to deal with fraud on a small and a large scale. The answers to this question varied based on the size of the organization staff and budget. Participant 7, who held the CPA designation and also had the largest budget, had the most comprehensive internal controls in place of all the participants. He stated "Leadership in his organization must disclose any conflict of interest. I do criminal background checks on everyone, especially for those who climb the rank of leadership." He states that as CEO, he reviews anything that directly affects the organization's bottom line and dollar limits. The company has liability insurance on various areas fraud may impact.

Participant 2 presented her observations of her organization's internal accounting controls by stating everyone is aware their entities books and financial statements are regularly reviewed. Participant 5 stated all money flow has oversight by more than one person at any given time. Participant 9 said she had no fraud mechanisms in place to deal with massive fraud. She continued that because of the size of their budget and staff she did not believe her entity was a target for massive fraud or theft. Ninety percent (90%) of all leaders had some internal controls to deal with fraud on a small or significant level. One or 10% had no internal controls. Two or 20% of RNPOs had an elaborate internal control model. Seventy percent (70%) had a very rudimentary or almost nonexistent internal control system.

The findings of this study validate what some studies purported that one of the universal variables in asset misappropriation and fraud in non-profit organizations is the accounting system's internal controls were deficient or did not exist to detect and deter fraud. For example, internal controls within nonprofit organizations are especially inadequate (Archambeault & Webber, 2018; Fitzgerald et al., 2018).

Feelings About Ability to Detect and Deter Fraud

Questions 12 and 20 related to an organizations ability to detect and deter fraud. Do you feel that your religious enterprise is fully protected against fraud? Are you and your Board of directors satisfied with the organization's ability to detect and deter fraud? There were varying responses. Sixty percent (60%) of respondents said they do not believe they adequately protected their enterprises against fraud, and 40% said they think it fully protected them. The responses to if the leaders believe their board of directors were satisfied with their organization's ability to detect and deter fraud mirrored the previous answers, except Participant 7 said he was never asked that question and he was unsure what his board of director's perspective on the question was at this time. The responses again confirmed that RNPO administrators were concerned about their organization's welfare. However, only 40% of interviewees said they fully protected it against fraud. RNPOs are susceptible to fraud because of overconfidence that they will not be victimized and are in denial that fraud can happen in their organization (Peters, 2015). However, this study found 60% of RNPO leaders did not feel confident about their internal controls and felt they needed improvement. The varying responses showed a sharp divide in viewpoints based on what each leader determined in their mind gaps they may face in their internal controls.

Understanding and Implementing Accounting Principles

Questions 14 and 15 are interrelated and determined more accurately if the RNPOs understood generally accepted accounting practices (GAAP) or had heard about Financial Accounting Standards Board (FASB) standards for not-for-profit organizations. The researcher asked these questions to determine if interviewees understood what proper accounting practices were and if they understood there were industry accountings standards for RNPOs. Also, the questions were asked to determine if the RNPOs had implemented any of the basic FASB recommendations such as creating segregation of duties, annual CPA audits, and checks and balances of bookkeeping procedures. The purpose of this question was two-fold. First, it determined RNPO leaders' competency about GAAP and FASB, which was included in the findings for Research Question 1. Second, it determined whether leaders implemented any of

FASB's recommended internal controls, which relates to Research Question 2. Again, the leadership competency construct is leader abilities, skills, knowledge, and other attributes that are relevant for a leader's success in a particular job (Hughes et al., 2008).

Seventy percent (70%) or 7 out of the 10 leaders said they did not understand GAAP or FASBs regulations. Only the three with the largest budgets understood GAAP and FASB principles and regulations. Two of the three respondents were either a former financial administrator or a CFO. The researcher asked participants' Question 14, which is a three-part question. First, interviewees were asked if they were interested in implementing the accounting internal control measure of segregation of duties if not already in place. The second part of the question asked would leaders consider hiring a CPA or a qualified financial professional annually to audit the organization's financial statements. Finally, leaders were asked if they were interested in creating checks and balances of bookkeeping procedures to enhance financial stewardship? The responses of leaders varied. Forty percent (40%) of interviewees stated these practices were already in place. Participant 1 noted all but annual audits by a CPA or financial profession were in place. He said he would like to implement yearly audits by a CPA or financial professional.

Participant 4 similarly stated they would like to implement all, but cannot hire a CPA at this point. Participant 9 was only interested in creating segregation of duties for the accounting operations. The other 30% of respondents were interested in implementing all the suggested recommendations.

Der Wal et al. (2016) found with various types of integrity and ethics training, it is limited unless it is targeted. Other than the two former CFO and financial administrators who were already familiar with GAAP and FASB, the other RNPO leaders were eager to understand and adopt some practices to better secure their organizations' financial resources. Harris et al. (2017) commented are amateurs in positions of governance in the stewardship of nonprofit organizations (NPO). The finding supports that many leaders may not quite understand the seriousness of fraud in their organizations and may need targeted training to develop their accounting competencies.

Control Activities

The researcher asked Question 16 to determine what control activities are in place by management to dissuade fraud, theft, and fraudulent activities? This question examined research question two a little further. Again, there were varying responses by RNPO leaders.

Participant 7 said that leadership must disclose any conflict of interest. I do criminal background checks on everyone. There are dollar limits on the amount anyone spends in the company. There is liability insurance in the event of theft. Participant 5 stated that all monies have oversight by over one person. Participant 3 said checks and balances are in place, and every receipt, over one person, must sign the receipt of monies and expenditure. All the other leaders, except one, said they had some variation of the three leaders above. Respondent 9 said they have no control activities because of the size of their entity's budget. There were polar results because each organization either had limited or extensive accounting controls to dissuade fraud in their organizations.

Fraud Committed by Leadership Versus by Non-Leadership

Participants were asked Question 17, 'What internal control does your organization have in place to deal with fraud committed by leadership versus fraud committed by non-leadership?' Fifty percent (50%) or five out of 10 RNPO leaders stated they did not have any internal control activities to deal with fraud committed by leaders versus non-leaders. Ten percent (10%) or one leader said their internal controls did not distinguish between leadership versus non-leadership. The same measure applies across the board. Participant 7 stated leadership must disclose conflict of interest. They do criminal background checks on everyone. As a person goes up the rank into administration, the CEO reviews things that directly impact the enterprise finances and accounting processes and there are dollar limits on what leadership can spend, and the company has liability insurance if there is any malfeasance by the administration.

Participant 3 stated the entity continuously reviews financial bank statements. Directors do not have the ability to transfer or write funds. Participant 6 expressed that in the local office, which he works for, it is a one-person operation. There are few transactions on the local level and multiple people at the national level overseeing the enterprise finances and accounting records.

Financial Transparency

Participants were asked Question 18, ‘How do you feel about the financial transparency of the organization?’ Eighty percent (80%) of the respondents stated that it satisfied them with the transparency of their organization. Twenty percent (20%) said their organization was not transparent. This question was important because it looked more closely at Research Question 2, and it aids all stakeholders, including leaders, to see if the internal accounting controls were working correctly. Ortega-Rodríguez et al. (2020) found that increasing the credibility of NPOs to raise the necessary funds reinforces the need to design and implement management and internal control systems capable of delivering the social and economic–financial information on the performance of the NPOs. Ortega-Rodríguez et al. (2020) continued “NPOs will be perceived as more credible if the information disclosed to their stakeholders is more transparent” (p. 16).

Risk Assessment

When asked Question 19, 'Describe whether your organization has ever done a risk assessment to determine its vulnerability to fraud,' 70% of respondents replied that a risk assessment was never done. Participant 7 said we required it as part of the entity's annual liability insurance application. He also stated their auditors did it to help the organization in assessing where it stands in its accounting records. The researcher designed this question to find out if an expert critically looked at the internal controls of the entity to determine if the organization's internal accounting controls properly worked, and what gaps, if any, exist in their enterprise controls. Based on the feedback, most of the entities needed to get a risk assessment done.

Feeling About Fraud Internally and Externally

Questions 21 and 22 were designed to elicit the feelings of how RNPO leaders would respond to fraud committed internally by an employee or volunteer. In addition, the researcher wanted to determine how they would feel when they heard about fraud against RNPOs externally, and how they viewed their internal controls after hearing about incidents of fraud against RNPOs.

When asked Question 21, 'Describe how you would respond to acts of fraud, waste, mismanagement, abuse, or misappropriation in the organization as an enterprise leader,' 90% of the leaders said it would disappoint them knowing the person who committed the fraud and abuse or mismanagement worked in their organization. Only 10% or one other leader noted because of the size of their budget and their organization's size, fraud or mismanagement would not happen in their enterprise. However, how each would handle the matter differed. Fifty percent (50%) of the RNPO leaders said they would immediately end the individual's employment who was caught in the impropriety. Leader 4 and leader 10 noted that before taking action to terminate the employee's employment, they would want to meet with the individual or individuals to determine why they committed this act against their entity. If there was not a plausible explanation, then they would terminate the employee or volunteer. Participant 8 goes a little further, stating he would do an introspection of himself to find out how he could have overlooked that person's poor character to put them in such a position of authority. Respondent 7 indicated if fraud was detected, his organization would immediately protect the data, use a forensic accountant, and discuss it with the audit committee. Disciplinary action would be taken and depending on how egregious the fraud was, it might be reported to external law enforcement authorities. A report would be submitted to the RNPO insurers and/or those with contractual obligations. Finally, the organizations leaders would determine why the fraud was not detected.

When asked Question 22, When you hear about fraudulent actions against the religious organization, how do you feel, and do these stories cause you to look at your current internal control,' 90% of interviewees stated it made them feel bad, horrible, disappointed, or grievous. Only one or 10% of the interviewees said she thinks there are three sides to the story, and she does not believe everything she hears about stories. Participant 8 said, "Yes, it makes my blood boil, and it elicits why you made it easy." He continues that a wise man said that pay me enough that I will not steal.

Sound Financial Stewardship and Final Comments

The interviewer designed Questions 23 and 25 to find out if there was any other information that respondents wanted to share that promote sound financial stewardship in securing the entity's resources. One or 10% of respondents said there is nothing else they would like to share regarding sound fiscal stewardship. One or 10% of interviewees said the interview was an eye-opening experience. Participant 10 said she believes her organization needs to be updated on tax laws and have someone to monitor their finances and accounting. Participant 8 stated that to promote sound financial stewardship, organizations need to ensure proper systems are in place. Leaders are well vetted through a skills test and to get licensed, bonded certified professionals to handle outsourcing. Participant 3 said organizations need to keep looking at controls to strengthen soft spots. Participant 6 stated as it pertains to churches that churches need prudence hiring CPAs and attorneys and having proper safeguards in place. Participant 7 said there is a tendency in Christian organizations to believe we are all nice and God-fearing people. However, he hopes each organization has tight controls in place. Overall, each participant voiced various gaps and needs they have in their organizations. Only one interviewee was relatively satisfied because she said they did not get enough funds to be concerned.

Relationship of Themes/Patterns to Research Questions

After one month of interviewing RNPO leaders in New Jersey, there were a few themes and perceptions revealed. The study findings are summarized according to four themes:

1. A critical factor that determined if RNPO leaders had internal accounting controls in place was awareness and perception of fraud.
2. Formal higher education alone is not a determinant for detecting and deterring fraud.
3. Specific training is inherently better to understand internal controls and fraud detection and deterrence.
4. Finally, in most cases, the size and budget of the RNPOs determined the level internal accounting controls were in place.

The first theme established in the finding was the lack of awareness of the dangers of fraud in RNPOs were critical in the detection of fraud. When the researcher asked if they feel they had anything to detect fraud, 90% of the interviewees said some type of internal control in place. Ten percent (10%) or one respondent had nothing in place. Of the 90%, 60% had little internal controls in place and the other 30% had a more robust system in position. Participant 4 expressed that the interview "was an eye-opening experience." Participant 10 who pastored her church for 5 years, said though she had an MBA and Ph.D., she never considered the issue of fraud and she had a lot of work to do after our interview. The finding of this research shows many of the leaders' interviewed were not aware and perceived that fraud was a potential problem that could impact their organizations. Peters (2015) found "a consistent finding in the research was that religious organizations, particularly smaller ones, tend to lack adequate internal controls and spiritual, not financial, matters are a priority in the organization to leaders of these organizations."

The second theme revealed in this study was formal higher education alone is not a determinant for detecting and deterring fraud. The finding of this study found the RNPOs leader interviewed in New Jersey was highly educated and 80% of them had a bachelor's degree or higher. The most educated respondent, Participant 10, had a Ph.D. and an MBA, but did not have any internal accounting controls because she did not perceive the importance of having it in place. Whereas when internal controls were discussed with Participant 8, he stated he had a bachelor's degree, and also had a thorough internal accounting control system in place, including having a CPA to conduct an annual risk assessment. So formal education by itself was not a 'silver bullet' empowering RNPO leaders in their effort of detecting and deterring fraud in their organizations. The findings show it must be coupled with awareness and perception of the risk of potential fraud in their entities. This study, in part, supports previous findings. Peters (2015) concluded in her findings that religious organizations possess unique vulnerabilities that make them susceptible to fraud because they are very trusting of individuals and give financial responsibilities to individuals who do not have the proper qualifications to handle such tasks. In this study, 80% of the leaders had bachelor's degrees or higher, but only 30% had significant accounting training and experience.

Another perception revealed during this study was 90% of interviewees believed additional training would help them better understand internal controls in their ability to deter and detection of fraud. Thomson et al. (2016) noted participants in their research showed ongoing training had improved their ability to understand the results. Nzinga, McGivern, and English (2019) suggested developmental and ongoing professional training significantly impacts how leaders enact their roles.

The final theme realized during the interviews was the smaller the staff and size of the budget, the more likelihood for the RNPO not to have any internal controls to deal with fraud. This confirms previous studies that larger religious organizations used more internal controls. Presumably, these organizations have more resources that enable employment of individuals with more excellent knowledge of finances and to hire outside consultants to recommend internal control (Peters, 2015; Wooten et al., 2003). The only outlier to this were two organizations that had parent operations. The parent organization provided the oversight from its home base though the local New Jersey operations were one-person units.

Summary of the Findings

This multi-case qualitative study explored if there was a relationship between leadership competence, perception, leadership style, and fraud detection and if RNPOs leaders have mechanisms or internal accounting controls to prevent accounting fraud. Overall, the general findings showed 10 diverse New Jersey RNPOs with highly educated leaders. The RNPOs staff sizes ranged from one person to 727 people. Their budgets ranged from $7,000 to $80 million.

There are a few revelations of the study that either refuted previous studies or confirmed other studies. This study revealed that 80% of all leaders had a bachelor's degree or higher. In fact, 70% had at least a master's degree. However, there was no conclusive evidence pointing towards that higher education by itself enables RNPO leaders to detect and deter fraud in their organizations.

However, after delving more in-depth, the study found 30% had obtained both specific higher education and/or experience on their job that prepared them to implement sound internal controls to detect and deter fraud. The finding also confirmed previous research that larger organizations are more likely to have a greater capacity to implement strategies that ensure access to vital resources such as critical staffing for survival and growth of the organization (Davis & Cobb, 2009; Del Mar Gálvez-Rodríguez et al., 2016). The organization with larger budgets and staff had paid leaders with more robust internal controls in place. Unanimously, all leaders believed they were responsible for the fiduciary oversight of their respective organization's resources. However, they all thought they needed training to get a better grasp of various financial and accounting issues that may influence their organizations.

Applications to Professional Practice

There are a few areas where this study can contribute to professional practice besides adding to the existing body of literature about the inability of leaders of RNPOs in New Jersey to identify and implement adequate accounting internal controls to detect and deter accounting fraud. Albrecht et al. (2015) cited that financial statement fraud is ordinarily a top-down type of fraud that adversely influences individuals, organizations, and society. Previous studies identified that detecting and deterring fraud in not-for-profit organizations should not be a secondary process, but an integral part of operations. The discovery of fraud often is costly and can have serious ramifications, possibly crippling an organization and potentially causing some entities to fail (Said et al., 2018).

Considering these threats, the first area that this multi-case qualitative study brings to light is the necessity for RNPOs founders, Board of Directors, and leaders to craft awareness and perception in their organizations' management and staff that the threat of fraud exists. After creating the awareness of fraud, management needs to provide recommendations and mechanisms to detect and deter it. In this study, many leaders did not consider the danger of fraud in their organization. Sixty percent (60%) of respondents said they did not believe they adequately protected their enterprises against fraud. Participant 10 of the study who holds a Ph.D. and MBA stated, "There is a lot of work that I need to do because I never consider issues surrounding fraud in my organization." Participant 4 said that the interview was "eye-opening," meaning she did not consider the threat of fraud in her organization.

In addition, 70% of RNPOs acknowledge they have nothing to deal with fraud potentially committed by leaders. The necessity of improving RNPOs leadership awareness can reduce its susceptibility to fraud schemes by implementing robust internal accounting controls to mitigate deficiencies. RNPOs can create and enhance the segregation of duties and develop inexperienced leaders and staff to devote the necessary resources to accounting functions (Gartland, 2016). This study revealed there is a lack of awareness and the need to educate RNPOs leaders about the implication of fraud in organizations.

Another finding identified in this study that can close gaps in fraud deterrence and detection in RNPOs is the use of trained financial professionals or CPAs. Seventy percent (70%) of respondents of the study expressed their organization has never done a risk assessment. Also, 70% or 7 out of the 10 leaders said they do not understand GAAP or FASBs regulations. Thousands of CPAs work in the not-for-profit sector, and thousands more volunteer as members of the governing boards of nonprofit organizations (Cashwell et al., 2019). CPAs and accountants provide valuable services because they inspect financial records to determine what story the financial records communicate to all stakeholders.

Besides laboriously going through financial records, CPAs and financial professionals perform risk assessments for RNPOs and other organizations to assist them in tightening their internal controls and identifying red flags in employees and financial records. Kummer et al. (2015) opined in their research that entities often use specific fraud assessment instruments and will find there are assortments of fraud detection and prevention tools available to them. Only 30% of the RNPOs in this study have ever done a risk assessment. A risk assessment would educate leaders where to start in closing the exposed gaps by would-be fraudsters. Also, trained professionals like CPAs can conduct a risk assessment. External CPA firms are also a valuable resource in conducting risk assessments to determine if an RNPO needs to invest a small or an extensive amount of resources in strengthening its current position against fraud.

Biblically, Jesus points out in Mark 13: 33-37 The Message translation:

> It's like a man who takes a trip, leaving home and putting his servants in charge, each assigned a task, and commanding the gatekeeper to stand watch. So, stay at your post, watching. You do not understand when the homeowner is returning, whether evening,

midnight, cockcrow, or morning. You don't want him showing up unannounced, with you asleep on the job. I say it to you, and I'm saying it to all: Stay at your post. Keep watch.

In addition to that, Luke 11: 39 The Message translation admonishes, "You know that if the house owner had known what night the burglar was coming, he wouldn't have stayed out late and left the place unlocked. So, don't you be slovenly and careless."

RNPOs leaders could glean from these passages of scriptures by staying alert and watchful if they need to provide an accurate accounting of resources to stakeholders. The fiduciary responsibility of RNPOs donations and grants to perform philanthropic acts ultimately rests on their shoulders. Luke 11, Jesus admonishes believers and gatekeepers to be careful and to watch or guard diligently. Thieves or burglars do announce their entrance. Gatekeeper or leaders must work to conscientiously protect and provide oversight so they can account for everything. Through internal controls and awareness, leaders can provide an accurate accounting of assets. Moody and Achenbaum (2014) posited that leaders should pursue earnestly to preserves and protect God's creation as faithful stewards.

The third significant finding this study revealed was leaders' need of ongoing training. Unlike professions like CPAs and attorneys, RNPO leaders do not have to take continuing education classes to maintain a professional license. Ongoing professional development is optional. Overwhelmingly, most of the RNPOs leaders in this study acknowledged the need for training about fraud, not-for-profit taxes, and cybersecurity pertain to their accounting and financial processes. Hauser (2019) suggested that employees' regular training is one of the most effective ways of preventing corruption. He continued in his argument that training must be specific to confront challenging questions regarding the gray areas of ethics and compliance. Thus, training can be a low-cost part of RNPOs' fight against fraud. In sum, the implementation of mechanisms to raise fraud awareness, hiring CPAs or financial professionals, and completing a risk assessment and training employees can aid RNPOs in their plight of guarding God's precious resources.

Recommendations for Action

Throughout this study it became apparent to the researcher there are very few differences between RNPOs and not-for-profit or for-profit organizations financially. The only thing that distinguishes RNPOs is the underlying tenets of faith that are subtly or noticeably interwoven in their mission and daily operations. Yasmin et al. (2014) opined that RNPOs are churches, nonprofit employers, civic organizations, or any organizations that hold some type of religious underpinning or faith in their core beliefs. In this research, RNPOs could incorporate if not already applied in their organization the following best practices.

- Raising fraud awareness
- Engaging a CPA or qualified financial profession to audit financial statements annually
- The creation of a fraud policy
- Require all administrators and key staff to attend annual or monthly training
- The annual review of financial policies with key members of staff.

Raising Fraud Awareness

One revelation doing the fieldwork was listening to the different perceptions of leaders of RNPOs in New Jersey about fraud. Participant 10, who had a Ph.D. and an MBA, stated that even though she had an MBA, which included some accounting education, she did not have any internal controls. She went on to express during our interview, she did not see the importance of having internal controls until after our interview. Creating awareness in RNPOs leadership is of extreme importance in the detection and deterring fraud. Fraud awareness should not be trivial, but ethical examples set by the administration within an organization will influence members' awareness of, and attitudes toward, codes of ethics, including fraud (Gates et al., 2016).

Continuous impromptu independent checks and balances can also serve as a psychological deterrent to perpetrators that everyone is being looked at on an interval basis. McMahon et al. (2016) suggested that the creation of a checks and balances system designed to ensure executives and employees are vigilant in an organization tactics of fighting financial crimes.

Engaging a CPA

To strengthen RNPOs financial statements and promote healthy accounting practice, including strong internal controls, leaders of RNPOs could employ the services of CPAs. One way to create awareness is to hire a forensic accountant or CPA to discuss crafting a roadmap and the implications of fraud with RNPOs leaders, especially the board of directors. A couple of the interviewees stated they would like to hire a CPA, but they did not have the funds. However, one of the most inexpensive ways to get an accountant or CPA is to elect one on the organization's board of directors (Harris et al., 2017). Jensen (1993) posited that the board of directors is the apex of the governance structure and as having ultimate responsibility for the effectiveness of the organization in which it serves (Harris et al., 2017). Jensen (1993) continued,

> Board monitoring involves regular oversight to ensure the charity has sufficient resources and systems to remain accountable to its various stakeholders. Board monitoring can reduce the likelihood of asset diversions in two ways. First, periodic reviews of financial reports and mission-related activities allow boards to detect potential problems sooner.

> Second, monitoring typically includes assessing, and if necessary, correcting, the organization's internal control system. Strong internal controls help prevent asset diversions. (p. 151)

So, reaching out to CPA societies or organizations such as the Black CPAs of America can be a source where Board of Directors can recruit a CPA. Board of Directors can reach out to colleagues in their field too for CPA references. Besides electing a CPA or financial professional on the Board of Directors, some CPAs volunteer their services to not for profit organizations, including religious ones. Shafer and Park (1999) pointed out that some CPAs provide pro-bono accounting services through not-for-profit groups such as Accountants for the Public Interest (API). API is a nonprofit organization whose emphasis is to encourage accountants to volunteer their time and expertise to individuals, small businesses, and nonprofits, who cannot afford professional accounting services.

The Creation of a Fraud Policy

Another best practice that RNPOs could consider in their effort to bolster their detection and deterrence is creating a fraud policy. A RNPO can create a comprehensive written fraud policy that all employees and volunteers sign at the start of their employment. Tiwari and Debnath (2017) found framing organizational-level policies such as a fraud policy that requires written acknowledgement from employees and volunteers that they have read and understood the clauses can be an effective fraud deterrent. Having each employee sign a written policy that they may be imprisoned can be a psychological deterrent in the mind of fraudsters. One way that RNPO leaders can design a fraud policy is by consulting with a financial professional or CPA. Apart from providing auditing services, CPA firms provide consultation services such as completing a risk assessment of internal controls and developing fraud policies. Besides that, leaders in these organizations could refer to accounting groups such as the association of fraud examiners (ACFE) who usually publish the Small Business Fraud Prevention Manuals. These manuals have samples of fraud policies and code of ethics that leaders of RNPOs can glean form to develop their fraud policies (Anders, 2020).

RNPOs could collaborate and become members of recognized organizations that may have a fraud policy template. Organizations like the Evangelical Christian Financial Accountability (ECFA) can provide RNPOs leaders with a trove of resources in developing their fraud policy. To give credibility to stakeholders (ECFA), RNPO leaders can follow some ECFA guidelines, stating that ECFA's Seven Standards of Responsible Stewardship, drawn from Scripture, are fundamental to operating with integrity. Accountability to God is vital, but people form their impressions of both people and organizations by looking at the outward appearances (1 Samuel 16:7; ECFA, 2020).

One best practice that RNPOs can adopted is training personnel. One need indicated by all the interviewees is the need for training. Campa (2018) found there is a direct correlation between the existence of fraud training and the reduction of financial statement manipulation. Training the board of directors, managers, and key personnel using workshops and seminars on the topic of fraud on a monthly quarter basis, but at least an annual can assist RNPOs in their plight to counteract fraud in their organization. Competent personnel can do internal training about the subject of fraud incorporating Biblical or religious context since most religions do not condone theft.

From a Biblical lens, leaders can use scriptures such as Ephesian 4: 28 New International Version (NIV). Anyone who has been stealing must steal no longer but must work, doing something useful with their own hands, that they may have something to share with those in need. If the organization does not have the resources or personnel to conduct internal training. In that case, they can use local face-to-face workshops, or seminars led by larger organizations in their sector or accounting associations such as (ACFE). Finally, training can be done using webinars or online or digital tools. Whether RNPOs do internal training, online, or by external entity research shows that having some fraud training helps mitigate challenges that organizations face with protecting its valuable resources.

Annual Review of Financial Policies

The final recommended best practice is reviewing fraud policies with key personnel at least annually to determine its effectiveness and appropriateness. With the constant changes in the business environment, systems need to be revised from time to time to see if it is current and useful. Essential personnel can set aside time revisiting fraud policies looking at the data together, exchanging ideas of what changes need to be made and creating strategies to make it current and useful. Prudent RNPO leaders can implement fraud awareness training among its staff and volunteers. RNPOs leader can engage a CPA to assist with developing fraud policies. Requiring key personnel to obtain fraud training and reviewing its fraud policy annually to make their businesses better in the deterrence and detection of fraud. Based on the respondents' feedback, the researcher determined that RNPOs can adopt all or some of the suggestions as best practices.

Recommendations for Further Study

There are few areas that researchers can expand upon to close some of the gaps in the study of the inability of leaders of religious not-for-profit organizations in New Jersey to identify and implement adequate accounting internal controls to detect and deter accounting fraud. Incidentally, all the RNPOs interviewed were philosophically Christian. One recommendation for further study for other researchers to explore is they could focus on other religious not for profits such as Sikhs, Hindus, Jews, and Muslims, to name a few religious RNPOs in New Jersey. Awang (2019) researched "fraud in financial reporting among Muslim participants" (p. 771). Awang's (2019) research shows that fraud does not discriminate against the type of religious organizations that it impacts.

Another idea for other researchers to expand on this research is to expand it to different geographic regions. The researcher could replicate this study in another state in the United States of America or even other countries outside of the United States, such as Canada, the United Kingdom, or China. Because of the globalization of economies, some issues such as fraud in RNPOs may creep into other societies. Malaysia, as an emerging country with a make-up of people of various religious persuasion and ethnic origin, is not without financial fraud (Nasir et al., 2019). So, replicating this study in another geographic region may benefit the population in that area.

An additional research area that inquisitive researchers may have an interest in exploring is a quantitative version of this study. This study investigated a multi-case study qualitative viewpoint of the inability of leaders in RNPOs to identify and implement adequate accounting controls. Quantitative studies can produce different result because it looks typically at a larger sample. Creswell (2015) pointed out that quantitative research is more narrowly focused on variables and looks at a sample with the intent to generalize from the sample.

Future research can examine the relationship between unorthodox accounting practices and fraud in religious not-for-profit organizations. Not all RNPOs may follow the General Accepted Accounting Principles (GAAP) or Financial Accounting Standards Board (FASB) internal accounting documents, practices, or operational processes. An organization may have adopted unorthodox accounting practices. Xu et al. (2016) reported between the period between 1986 and 1997, the use of a non-GAAP system of measurement sharply increased in the United States. A researcher may look at the use of non- GAAP methods used by RNPOs and its relationship to fraud.

An additional recommendation for further research is the use of other methods of protecting the organization's assets. In recent years, organizations have implemented management information systems to act as the proverbial sixth man in their fight against fraud. Many organizations promote paying electronically via PayPal and Cash app, both electronic management information payment systems. Some technologically savvy fraudsters may find a way to divert funds using these payment methods to their personal accounts. Segal (2016) pointed out that the explosion of computer-based resources opened the portal for a new kind of computer-based accounting fraud. A researcher may provide valuable information on how to assist organizations in securing this area of fraud that may occur in RNPOs.

The last area that other researchers may be interested in exploring how RNPOs can strengthen their internal controls is already in place against external fraud risk and fraud committed solely by management. One variable in Cressey's fraud triangle theory is the opportunity. Management often time are in ideal positions to take advantage of RNPOs. Zuberi and Siasa (2019) acknowledged that not for profits are faced with internal criminological factors management collusion with third-party vendors and management internal control overrides. A study examining whether RNPOs have adequate internal controls to deal with managerial fraud could be considered. The areas mentioned above area are certain things that an interested researcher could assess in the future.

Reflections

As a born-again believer, I have worked in multiple professions throughout my career. The exposure to various business sectors has allowed me to see several not-for-profit entities, including my local church, where I serve as a trustee and one of the assistant pastors. Coupled with that, studying for-profit and nonprofit management at the graduate and undergraduate level enabled me to conceptually and practically view these organizations. Students have often contacted me where I serve as an adjunct faculty and random people familiar with my background about starting an RNPO and fundraising. Fundraising many times seemly was their primary concern. Internal controls were no way on their radar of concerns. Therefore, my viewpoint before the study was that RNPOs are primarily small struggling entities with no direction or vision because of a lack of resources. I viewed most RNPOs entities as a person or people who had a passion or an interest in helping people because of some tragedy that they or their family or someone close to them went through. As a result of the tragedy, in attempt to make a difference these people created a RNPO or NPO as a way of giving back or attempting to cure some societal ills.

Nevertheless, as a rule of thumb, I am relatively objective unless I there is enough evidence sway my opinion in another direction. Ordinarily, I did not see RNPOs as multi-million-dollar operations other than the Red Cross, Salvation Army and a few other organizations. Though a few of RNPOs in the study fit my initial perception, to my surprise, some RNPOs were multi-million-dollar operations that have strong internal controls and well-educated and well-trained staff to lead the organization. One RNPO had an 80-million-dollar operation and another 2.75-million-dollar operation. In these organizations, the CEO was a former CPA, and in the other the executive director was a former financial administrator.

Another preconceived notion that I had was most RNPOs leaders were not very educated. Again, to my surprise, 70% of the interviewees had a master's degree or higher. The interview guide helped mitigate personal biases in that it was objective, and as a researcher, I believe I did not influence the outcome or the answers of participants.

Biblically, RNPO leaders need to realize that they may have God-inspired vision to help others in life, but like everything after the fall of Adam and Eve—people and things are broken. Van Duzer (2010) pointed out that broken people move from God-centeredness to me centeredness. Me-centered people find themselves in good organizations, and if the opportunity presents itself, they will commit fraud.

The Old Testament book of Nehemiah is a classic example of enemies of the work of God. Nehemiah started to rebuild the temple when he was faced with opposition from two enemies namely Sanballat and Tobiah. Nehemiah 4:21-23 (NIV) records,

So we continued the work with half the men holding spears, from the first light of dawn till the stars came out. At that time, I also said to the people, 'Have every man and his helper stay inside Jerusalem at night so that they can serve us as guards by night and as workers by day. Neither I nor my brothers nor my men nor the guards with me took off our clothes; each had his weapon, even when he went for water.'

In these passages of scripture, Nehemiah was focused on the mission of rebuilding the wall of Jerusalem, but he was also focused on defending the progress made. Sometimes RNPOs leaders ignore or are ignorant of the threats that face their organization and do not implement the necessary mechanisms to protect the resources they are entrusted with. Nehemiah's leadership is an excellent example of prudent leadership that one can focus on the mission, but simultaneously focus on threats such as fraud. This study revealed a need for RNPO leaders to remember the brokenness of human beings in their organizations.

Summary and Study Conclusions

In conclusion, this multi case qualitative study of the inability of leaders of religious not-for-profit organizations in the State of New Jersey to identify and implement adequate accounting internal controls to detect and deter accounting fraud was crafted to add to the limited body of literature on the subject. Archambeault and Webber (2018) opined there is a deficiency of pragmatic data on the consequences of fraud in NPOs even worse in RNPOs. The reality is fraud affects all organizations, even those that have religiosity at their core or sprinkled into their mission.

This multi-case qualitative study discussed the findings based on interviews with 10 diverse RNPO leaders in New Jersey concerning leadership competence, perception, leadership style, and mechanisms or internal accounting controls they had in place to prevent accounting fraud. The findings of the study both refuted and bolsters previous research. The findings of this study showed a highly educated group of leaders with 80% attaining a bachelor's degree or higher. Moreover, out of the 80%, 30% held a bachelor's or master's in business administration and/or CPA designation. Further, 2 or 20% of the 80% were either a financial administrator or CFO in their careers. Additional, 3 or 30% of the research respondents had a bachelor's or master's degree in business administration with credits in accounting. This finding refutes some previous research. Often, volunteers obtain little job training and many times are less credentialed (Steimel, 2018).

Another finding this study refuted is Harris et al. (2017), who pointed out there are amateurs in positions of governance in the stewardship of nonprofit organizations (NPO). This study showed the average amount of time each of the RNPOs leaders was employed in a leadership position in their organization was 50%, including both partially and fully paid employees. In part, this invalidated a previous study that many smaller NPOs may not have the relevant expertise and resources to prevent fraud and volunteers obtain little job training and many times are less credentialed (Kummer et al., 2015; Steimel, 2018).

One finding that validates previous studies is the need for specific and ongoing training. Overwhelmingly 90% or nine out of the participants interviewed indicated they needed additional training for various reason. This finding supports previous findings. Hauser (2019) suggested that regular training of employees is one of the most effective ways of preventing corruption. Der Wal et al. (2016) opined leaders would not benefit from various types of integrity and ethics training, unless it is targeted. Other than a former CFO and a former financial administrators who were already familiar with GAAP and FASB, the other RNPO leaders were eager to obtain additional training to better secure their organizations' financial resources.

One of the discoveries in this study was the difference in perspective of fraud and internal controls. There was a polar opposite of opinions and perspectives primarily based on organizations budget and size. One interviewee expressed the interview was "an eye-opening experience." Another respondent, the highest educated with an MBA and Ph.D., stated her perception of fraud was she did not see the importance of internal controls. Another interviewee stated she did not see the importance of internal controls either in her organization because her organization did not have a large budget. However, the former CPA stated his organization had a robust internal control system and protecting his organization's assets was extremely important. However, there were two outliers to the summary of fraud awareness. These local entities had parent organizations that had healthy oversight of the local chapters' budget and finances. Based on the on the findings, it was clear that raising fraud awareness among RNPO leaders was essential in detecting and deterring fraud.

As it pertains to how the leaders felt about their organizations ability to protect against fraud, 60% of respondents stated they did not feel they were protected against fraud. Again, fraud was not a tremendous consideration in the operations of these RNPOs. To aid practitioners in their plights, the study provided a few recommendations for action. The first was creating a fraud awareness program in their organization by having employees sign the RNPOs fraud policy upon hire. Another suggestion was engaging a CPA by either employing one on the board of directors or hiring one or reaching out to CPA societies to get one through volunteerism. Two lesser, but equally important recommendations, were creating a fraud policy and conducting at least annual training with key employee and volunteers.

In closing, many RNPOs have selfless and beautiful people with lofty goals to help the world be a better place. However, like Nehemiah, besides focusing on the mission, RNPO leaders must stay vigilant and abreast of the threats that lurks in their organizations. Unfortunately, some employees and volunteers in their organization if the opportunity presents itself would siphon off funds for their selfish greed.

References

Akers, R. L., & Matsueda, R. L. (1989). Donald R. Cressey: An intellectual portrait of a criminologist. *Sociological Inquiry, 59*(4), 423–438. https://doi.org/10.1111/j.1475-682X.1989.tb00118.x

Albrecht, C., Holland, D., Malagueño, R., Dolan, S., & Tzafrir, S. (2015). The role of power in financial statement fraud schemes. *Journal of Business Ethics, 131*(4), 803–813. https://doi.org/10.1007/s10551-013-2019-1

Albrecht, W. S., Howe, K. R., & Romney, M. B. (1984). *Deterring fraud: The internal auditor's perspective.* The Institute of Internal Auditors' Research Foundation. https://searchworks.stanford.edu/view/10012299

Al-Halabi, N. B. (2018). The impact of applying modern financial analysis tools on detecting fraudulent practices in financial statements of listed banks - An analytical study. *Pertanika Journal of Social Sciences & Humanities, 26*(4), 2599–2612. https://search-ebscohost-com.ezproxy.liberty.edu/login.aspx?direct=true&db =hlh&AN=134106681&site=ehost-live&scope=site

Alpi, K., & Evans, J. J. (2019). Distinguishing case study as a research method from case reports as a publication type. *Journal of the Medical Library Association, 107*(1), 1–5. https://doi.org/10.5195/jmla. 2019.615

American Institute of Certified Public Accountants. (2018). *AU-C Section.* Retrieved from https://www.aicpa.org/Research/Standards/AuditAttest/DownloadableDocuments/AU-C-00315.pdf

Amiram, D., Bozanic, Z., Cox, J. D., Dupont, Q., Karpoff, J. M., & Sloan, R. (2018). Financial reporting fraud and other forms of misconduct: A multidisciplinary review of the literature. *Review of Accounting Studies*, *23*(2), 732–783. https://doi.org/10.1007/s11142-017-9435-x

Anders, S. B. (2020). ACFE and ABFA Fraud Resources. *CPA Journal*, *90*(3), 62–63. https://www.cpajournal.com/2020/04/21/acfe-and-abfa-fraud-resources/

Archambeault, D. S., & Webber, S. (2018). Fraud survival in nonprofit organizations: Empirical evidence. *Nonprofit Management and Leadership*, *29*(1), 29–46. https://doi.org/10.1002/nml.21313

Archambeault, D. S., Webber, S., & Greenlee, J. (2015). Fraud and corruption in U.S. nonprofit entities: *A Summary of Press Reports 2008-2011*, *44*(6), 1194–1224. https://doi.org/10.1177/0899764014555987

Arvidson, M., & Lyon, F. (2014). Social impact measurement and non-profit organizations: Compliance, resistance, and promotion. *Voluntas*, *25*(4), 869–886. https://doi.org/10.1007/s11266-013-9373-6

Association of Certified Fraud Examiners. (2019a). *Fraud resources*. Retrieved from https://www.acfe.com/fraud-101.aspx.

Association of Certified Fraud Examiners. (2019b). *Fighting Fraud in Government*. Retrieved from https://www.acfe.com/uploadedFiles/Shared_Content/Products/Self-Study_CPE/Fighting%20Fraud_Chapter.pdf.

Association of Certified Fraud Examiners. (2020). Retrieved https://acfepublic.s3-us-west-2.amazonaws.com/2020-Report-to-the-Nations.pdf.

Awang, Y. (2019). The influences of attitude, subjective norm and adherence to Islamic professional ethics on fraud intention in financial reporting. *Journal of Islamic Accounting and Business Research*, *10*(5), 710–725. https://doi.org/10.1108/JIABR-07-2016-0085

Azrina, M. Y., & Ling Lai, M. (2014). An integrative model in predicting corporate tax fraud. *Journal of Financial Crime*, *21*(4), 424–432. https://doi.org/10.1108/JFC-03-2013-0012

Backer, J. (2016). Thou shalt not electioneer religious nonprofit political activity and the threat "God pacs" pose to democracy and religion. *Michigan Law Review*, *114*(4), 619–648. https://repository.law.umich.edu/mlr/vol114/iss4/3

Baker, S. E., & Edwards, R. (2012). How many qualitative interviews is enough? Expert voices and early career reflections on sampling and cases in qualitative research. *National Centre for Research Methods Review Paper.* http://eprints.ncrm.ac.uk/2273/4/how_many_interviews.pdf.

Bandura, A. (1999). Moral disengagement in the perpetration of inhumanities. *Personality and Social Psychology Review*, *3*, 193–209. https://doi.org/10.1207/s15327957pspr0303_3

Barbuto, J. E., & Wheeler, D. W. (2006). Scale development and construct clarification of servant leadership. *Group Organization Management*, *31*(3), 300–326. https://doi.org/10.1177/1059601106287091

Bartlett, L., & Vavrus, F. (2017). *Rethinking case study research: a comparative approach.* Routledge.

Bernstein, R., Buse K., & Bilimoria, D. (2016). Revisiting agency and stewardship theories: Perspectives from nonprofit board chairs and CEOs. *Nonprofit Management and Leadership*, *26*(4), 489–498. https://doi.org/10.1002/291542-7854/issues

Bloomberg, L. D., & Volpe, M. (2012). *Completing your qualitative dissertation: A road map from beginning to end* (2nd ed.). Sage.

Børgesen, K., Nielsen, R. K., & Henriksen, T. D. (2016). Exploiting formal, non-formal and informal learning when using business games in leadership education. *Development and Learning in Organizations*, *30*(6), 16–19. https://doi.org/10.1108/DLO-06-2016-0046

Boyatzis, R. (1982). *The competent manager. A model for effective performance.* https://www.researchgate.net/publication/247813294_The_Competent_Manager_A_Model_For_Effective_Performance

Boyatzis, R. (Ed.). (2008). *Competencies in the 21st century: Competencies in the 21st century.* https://ebookcentral-proquest-com.ezproxy.liberty.edu

Campa, D. (2018). Regulatory enforcement and the effectiveness of fraud training: A European investigation into earnings manipulation. *Comptabilité Contrôle Audit*, *24*(1), 81–111. https://doi.org/10.3917/cca.241.0081

Cashwell, K., Copley, P., & Dugan, M. (2019). Using ratio analysis to manage not-for-profit organizations. *CPA Journal*, *89*(5), 52–57. https://www.cpajournal.com/2019/06/05/using-ratio-analysis-to-manage-not-for-profit-organizations/

Chandra, Y., & Shang, L. (2017). An RQDA-based constructivist methodology for qualitative research. *Qualitative Market Research: An International Journal*, *20*(1), 90–112. https://doi.org/10.1108/QMR-02-2016-0014

Charmaz, K. (2017). Special invited paper: continuities, contradictions, and critical inquiry in grounded theory. *International Journal of Qualitative Methods*, *16*(1), 1609406917719350. https://doi.org/10.1177/1609406917719350

Chen, L. (2018). The Sec's forgotten power of exemption: how the sec can receive deference in favor of internal whistleblowers even when the text is clear. *Emory Law Journal*, *67*(5), 1043–1075. https://law.emory.edu/elj/content/volume-67/issue-5/comments/sec-power-exemption-favor-whistleblowers.html

Clandinin, D. J. (2006). *Handbook of narrative inquiry: Mapping a methodology*. Sage.

Clandinin, J., Pushor, D., & Orr, A. M. (2007). Navigating sites for narrative inquiry. *Journal of Teacher Education*, *58*(1), 21–35. https://doi.org/10.1177/0022487106296218

Clarke, M., & Ware, V. A. (2015). Understanding faith-based organizations: How FBOs are contrasted with NGOs in international development literature. *Progress in Development Studies*, *15*(1), 37–48. https://doi.org/10.1177/1464993414546979

Colombo, R. J. (2017). The religious liberty jurisprudence of Justice Antonin Scalia. *Hofstra Law Review*, *46*(2), 433–443. https://www.hofstralawreview.org/wp-content/uploads/2018/03/bb.1.colombo.pdf

Committee of Sponsoring Organizations of the Treadway Commission (COSO). (2017). *Report of the national commission on fraudulent financial reporting.* http://www.Coso.org/Publications/NCFFR.pdf. Accessed August 2020.

Committee of Sponsoring Organizations of the Treadway Commission (COSO). (1987). *Report of the national commission on fraudulent financial reporting*. http://www. Coso.org/Publications/NCFFR.pdf. Accessed November 2018.

Committee of Sponsoring Organizations of the Treadway Commission. (1992). *Internal control integrated framework* Vol. 2. COSO.

Committee of Sponsoring Organizations of the Treadway Commission (COSO). (2013). I*nternal Control— Integrated Framework*. COSO.

Committee of Sponsoring Organizations (COSO). (2017). Enterprise Risk Management—Integrating with Strategy and Performance. Retrieved from www.coso.org.

Considine, M., O'Sullivan, S., & Nguyen, P. (2014). New public management and welfare-to-work in Australia: Comparing the reform agendas of the ALP and the Coalition. *Australian Journal of Political Science*, *49*(3), 469–485. https://doi.org/10.1080/10361146.2014.931343

Cooper, D. R., & Schindler, P. S. (2008). *Business research methods* (10th ed.). McGraw-Hill.

Corporate Works. (2014). *American Benedictine Review*, *65*(2), 124–125. https://www.americanbenedictinereview.org/

Crabtree, B. F., & Miller, W. L. (1999). *Doing qualitative research* (2nd ed.). Sage.

Cressey, D. R. (1953). *Other people's money: A study in the social psychology of embezzlement.* Free Press.

Creswell, J. W. (2015). *Research design: Qualitative, quantitative, and mixed methods approaches* (4th ed.). Sage.

Creswell, J. W. (2016). *30 essential skills for the qualitative researcher* (2nd ed.). Sage.

Creswell, J. W., & Poth, C. N. (2018). *Qualitative inquiry & research design: Choosing among five approaches* (4th ed.). Sage.

Crofts, K. (2014). What drives the construction of reports and other accountability mechanisms in Australian faith-based social service not-for-profit organizations? *Third Sector Review*, *20*(2), 57–78. https://search.informit.org/documentSummary;res=IELAPA;dn=956701092421225

Cruz, R. F., & Tantia, J. F. (2017). Reading and understanding qualitative research. *American Journal of Dance Therapy*, *39*(1), 79–92. https://doi.org/10.1007/s10465-016-9219-z

Daniel, B. K. (2018). Empirical verification of the "TACT" framework for teaching rigor in qualitative research methodology. *Qualitative Research Journal*, *18*(3), 262–275. https://doi.org/10.1108/QRJ-D-17-00012

D'Aquila, J. M. (2013). COSO's Internal Control--Integrated Framework. *CPA Journal*, *83*(10), 22–29. https://www.coso.org/Pages/ic.aspx

D'Aquila, J. M., & Houmes, R. (2014). COSO's updated internal control and enterprise risk management frameworks. *CPA Journal*, *84*(5), 54–59. https://www.coso.org

Dal Magro, C. B., & da Cunha, P. R. (2017). Red flags in detecting credit cooperative fraud: The perceptions of internal auditors. *Revista Brasileira De Gestão De Negócios*, *19*(65), 469–491. https://doi.org/10.7819/rbgn.v19i65.2918

Davis, G. F. & Cobb, J. A. (2009). Resource dependence theory: past and future. In Bacharach, S.B. (Ed.), *Research in the Sociology of Organizations* (pp. 21–42). Elsevier, London.

De Armond, L., & Zack, G. (2017). Assess your organization's vulnerability to fraud. *Nonprofit World*, *35*, 20–21. Retrieved from http://ezproxy.liberty.edu/login?url=https://search-proquest-com.ezproxy.liberty.edu/docview/1970110063?accountid=12085.

Dellaportas, S. (2013). Conversations with inmate accountants: Motivation, opportunity and the fraud triangle. *Accounting Forum*, *37*(1), 29–39. https://doi.org/10.1016/j.accfor.2012.09.003

Del Mar Gálvez-Rodríguez., M., Caba-Pérez, C., & López-Godoy, M. (2016). Drivers of twitter as a strategic communication tool for non-profit organizations. *Internet Research*, *26*(5), 1052–1071. https://doi.org/10.1108/IntR-07-2014-0188

Der Wal, Z., Graycar, A., & Kelly, K. (2016). See no evil, hear no evil? Assessing corruption risk perceptions and strategies of Victorian public bodies. *Australian Journal of Public Administration*, *75*(1), 3–17. https://doi.org/10.1111/1467-8500.12163

Dickins, D., & Fay, R. G. (2017). COSO 2013: Aligning internal controls and principles. *Issues in Accounting Education*, *32*(3), 117–127. https://doi.org/10.2308/iace-51585

DiMaggio, P. J., & Anheier, H. K. (1990). The sociology of nonprofit organizations and sectors. *Annual Review of Sociology*, *16*(1), 137–159. https://doi.org/10.2307/2083266

Dion, M. (2016). Agency theory and financial crime: The paradox of the opportunistic executive. *Journal of Financial Crime*, *23*(3), 574–587. https://doi.org/10.1108/JFC-03-2015-0012

Dixon, O. (2016). Honesty without fear? Whistleblower anti-retaliation protections in corporate codes of conduct. *Melbourne University Law Review*, *40*(1), 168–206. https://papers.ssrn.com/sol3/papers.cfm?abstract_id=2921688

Dong, W., Liao, S., & Zhang, Z. (2018). Leveraging financial social media data for corporate fraud detection. *Journal of Management Information Systems*, *35*(2), 461–487. https://doi.org/10.1080/07421222.2018.1451954

Donnelly, K. S. (2010). Good governance: Has the IRS usurped the business judgment of tax-exempt organizations in the name of transparency and accountability? *UMKC Law Review*, *79*(1), 163–193. https://heinonline.org/HOL/LandingPage?collection =journals&handle=hein.journals/umkc79&div=9&id=&page=

Dorminey, J., Fleming, A. S., Kranacher, M. J., & Riley Jr, R. A. (2012). The evolution of fraud theory. *Issues in Accounting Education*, *27*(2), 555–579. https://doi.org/10.2308/iace-50131

Dresser, R. (2013). Subversive subjects: Rule-breaking and deception in clinical trials. *Journal of Law, Medicine & Ethics*, *41*(4), 829–840. https://doi.org/10.1111/jlme.12093.

ECFA. (2020). *ECFA's Integrity Standards for Nonprofits*. Retrieved on July 28, 2020 from https://www.ecfa.org/Standards.aspx

Ellis, T. J., & Levy, Y. (2009). Towards a guide for novice researchers on research methodology: Review and proposed methods. *Issues in Informing Science & Information Technology*, *6*, 323–337. https://doi.org/10.28945/1062

Elson, R., Callaghan, J. O., Walker, S., & John, P. (2007). Corporate governance in religious organization: A study of current practices in the local church. *Academy of Accounting and Financial Studies Journal*, *11*(1), 121–130. https://www.questia.com/library/journal/1G1-182468626/corporate-governance-in-religious-organizations-a

Enofe, A., & Amaria, P. (2011). The role of the church denomination in financial accountability among religious organizations. *International Journal of Business, Accounting, & Finance*, *5*(2), 87–104. http://search.ebscohost.com.ezproxy.liberty.edu/login.aspx?direct=true&db=bth&AN=69616363&site=ehost-live&scope=site.

Erasmus, B., & Morey, P. J. (2016). Faith-based volunteer motivation: Exploring the applicability of the volunteer functions inventory to the motivations and satisfaction levels of volunteers in an Australian faith-based organization. *Voluntas*, *27*(3), 1343–1360. https://doi.org/10.1007/s11266-016-9717-0

Eraut, M. (2004). Informal learning in the workplace. *Studies in Continuing Education*, *26*(2), 247–273. https://doi.org/10.1080/15803704200022524

Feng, N. C., Daniel, G. N., & Slatten, L. A. D. (2019). Stakeholder groups and accountability accreditation of non-profit organizations. *Journal of Public Budgeting, Accounting & Financial Management*, *31*(2), 218–236. https://doi.org/10.1108/JPBAFM-08-2018-0088

Festinger, L. A. (1957). *A theory of cognitive dissonance*. Peterson.

Financial Accounting Standards Board (FASB). (2016). *Accounting standards update* (No. 2016 14). https://www.fasb.org/jsp/FASB/FASBContent_C/Completed ProjectPage &cid =1176168381520.

Fitzgerald, B. C., Omer, T. C., & Thompson, A. M. (2018). Audit partner tenure and internal control reporting quality: U.S. evidence from the not-for-profit sector. *Contemporary Accounting Research*, *35*(1), 334–364. https://doi.org/10.1111/1911-3846.12348

Fitzsimons, A. P., McCarthy, I. N., & Silliman, B. R. (2018). FASB issues new guidance to improve financial reporting for not-for-profit organizations. *Review of Business*, *38*(1), 36–46. https://www.fasb.org/cs/ContentServer?c=FASBContent_C&cid =1176170797011&d=Touch&pagename=FASB%2FFASBContent_C%2FNewsPage

France, A., & Tang, W. (2018). Stakeholder accountability of a non-profit organisation subsidiary. *New Zealand Journal of Applied Business Research*, *16*(1), 19–33. https://search.informit.com.au/documentSummary;dn=552491935593475;res=IELNZC;type=pdf

Frazer, L. (2016). Internal control: Is it a benefit or fad to small companies? A literature dependency perspective. *Journal of Accounting and Finance*, *16*(4), 149–161. http://www.na-businesspress.com/JAF/FrazerL_Web16_4_.pdf

Fredriksen, P. (2014). Paul's Letter to the Romans, the ten commandments, and pagan "justification by faith." *Journal of Biblical Literature*, *133*(4), 801–808. https://doi.org/10.15699/jbibllite.133.4.801

Fusch, P. I., & Ness, L. R. (2015). Are we there yet? Data saturation in qualitative research. *Qualitative Report*, *20*(9), 1408–1416. http://www.nova.edu/ssss/QR/QR20/9/fusch1.pdf

Gamble, E., & Beer, H. (2017). Spiritually informed not-for-profit performance measurement. *Journal of Business Ethics*, *141*(3), 451–468. https://doi.org/10.1007/s10551-015-2682-5

Gao, L., & Brink, A. G. (2017). Whistleblowing studies in accounting research: A review of experimental studies on the determinants of whistleblowing. *Journal of Accounting Literature*, *38*, 1–13. https://doi.org/10.1016/j.acclit.2017.05.001

Gardner, H. (2000). A case against spiritual intelligence. *International Journal for the Psychology of Religion*, *10*(1), 27–34. https://doi.org/10.1207/S15327582IJPR1001_3

Gartland, D. J. (2016). Risks of not-for-profit and government audits. *Journal of Accountancy*, *221*(4), 16–18. https://www.journalofaccountancy.com/issues/2016/apr/auditing-not-for-profits-and-government.html#:~:text=This%20may%20lead%20to%20the,firm %2C%20citing%20the%20audit%20failure.

Gates, S., Prachyl, C. L., & Sullivan, C. (2016). Using report to the nations on occupational fraud and abuse to stimulate discussion of fraud in accounting and business classes. *Journal of Business and Behavioral Sciences*, *28*(1), 106–115. http://asbbs.org/files/2016/JBBS_28.1_Spring_2016.pdf#page=107

Geer, B. W., Maher, J. K., & Cole, M. T. (2008). Managing nonprofit organizations: The importance of transformational leadership and commitment to operating standards for nonprofit accountability. *Public Performance & Management Review, 32*(1), 51–75. https://doi.org/10.2753/PMR1530-9576320103

Gelling, L. (2015). Stages in the research process. *Nursing Standard, 29*(27), 44. https://doi.org/10.7748/ns.29.27.44.e8745

Gerard, J. A., & Weber, C. M. (2014). How agency theory informs a $30 million fraud. *Journal of Finance, Accounting & Management*, *5*(1), 16–47. https://www.semanticscholar.org/paper/How-Agency-Theory-Informs-a-%2430-Million-Fraud-Gerard-Weber/cf361696f6dfb726116779daf0c6ddc79a8cc51e

Gibson, M. (2018). *An analysis of fraud prevention and detection in not-for-profit organizations in the state of South Carolina* (Doctoral dissertation, Liberty University). https://digitalcommons.liberty.edu/cgi/viewcontent.cgi?article=2857&context=doctoral

Giving USA. (2017). The annual report on philanthropy for the year 2016: *Indiana University Lilly family school of philanthropy*. Giving USA Foundation.

Giving USA. (2018). *The annual report on philanthropy for the year 2016: Indiana University Lilly family school of philanthropy*. Giving USA Foundation.

Gramling, A., & Schneider, A. (2018). Effects of reporting relationship and type of internal control deficiency on internal auditors' internal control evaluations. *Managerial Auditing Journal*, *33*(3), 318–335. https://doi.org/10.1108/MAJ-07-2017-1606.

Gratton, P. C. (2018). Organization development and strategic planning for non-profit organizations. *Organization Development Journal*, *36*(2), 27–38. http://ezproxy.liberty.edu/login?qurl=https%3A%2F%2Fsearch.proquest.com%2Fdocview%2F2099388933%3Faccountid%3D12085

Gregory, E. M. (2017). *Exploring cash fraud awareness in nonprofit organizations* (Publication No. 1884346964) [Doctoral dissertation, Capella University). ProQuest Dissertations & Theses Global.

Guidestar. (2020). *Directory of charities and non-profit organizations*. https://www.guidestar.org/NonprofitDirectory.aspx?cat=8&subcat=44&p=1

Hager, M. A., & Hedberg, E. C. (2016). Institutional trust, sector confidence, and charitable giving. *Journal of Nonprofit & Public Sector Marketing*, *28*(2), 164–184. https://doi.org/10.1080/10495142.2015.1011508

Harris, E., Petrovits, C., & Yetman, M. H. J. J. (2017). Why bad things happen to good organizations. *The Link between Governance and Asset Diversions in Public Charities*, *146*(1), 149–166. https://doi.org/10.1007/s10551-015-2921-9.

Hauser, C. (2019). Fighting against corruption: Does anti-corruption training make any difference? *Journal of Business Ethics*, *159*(1), 281–299. https://doi.org/10.1007/s10551-018-3808-3

Hayashi Jr, P., Abib, G., & Hoppen, N. (2019). Validity in qualitative research: A processual approach. *The Qualitative Report*, *24*(1), 98–112. https://nsuworks.nova.edu/tqr/vol24/iss1/8/

Haynes, J. (2009). Conflict, conflict resolution and peacebuilding: The role of religion in Mozambique, Nigeria and Cambodia. *Commonwealth & Comparative Politics*, *47*, 52–75. https://doi.org/10.1080/14662040802659033

Hemraj, M. B. (2004). Preventing corporate scandals. *Journal of Financial Crime*, *11*(3), 268-276. https://doi.org/10.1108/13590790410809202

Hou, J., Zhang, C., & King, R. A. (2017). Understanding the dynamics of the individual donor's trust damage in the philanthropic sector. *Voluntas*, *28*(2), 648–671. https://doi.org/10.1007/s11266-016-9681-8

Houdek, P. (2017). Professional identity and dishonest behavior. *Society*, *54*(3), 253–260. https://doi.org/10.1007/s12115-017-0132-y

Huang, S. Y., Lin, C. C., Chiu, A. A., & Yen, D. C. (2017). Fraud detection using fraud triangle risk factors. *Information Systems Frontiers*, *19*(6), 1343–1356. https://doi.org/10.1007/s10796-016-9647-9

Huber, W. D. (2017). Forensic accounting, fraud theory, and the end of the fraud triangle. *Journal of Theoretical Accounting Research*, *12*(2), 28–49. https://ssrn.com/abstract=2423809

Hymel, G. (2006.). *Research methods for massage and holistic therapies.* Elsevier Mosby.

Isa, T. (2011). Impacts and losses caused by the fraudulent and manipulated financial information on economic decisions. *Review of International Comparative Management / Revista de Management Comparat International*, *12*(5), 929–939. http://search.ebscohost.com.ezproxy.liberty.edu/login.aspx?direct=true&db=bth&AN=71159723&site=ehost-live&scope=site

Isaksson, A. S. (2015). Corruption along ethnic lines: A study of individual corruption experiences in 17 African countries. *Journal of Development Studies*, *51*(1), 80–92. https://doi.org/10.1080/00220388.2014.947282

Jackson, S. L. (2015). The vexing problem of defining financial exploitation. *Journal of Financial Crime*, *22*(1), 63–78. https://doi.org/10.1108/JFC-05-2014-0026

Jacobs, J. A. (1954). Other people's money. A study in the social psychology of embezzlement. *Journal of Criminal Law, Criminology & Police Science*, *45*(4), 464–465. https://doi.org/10.2307/1140029

Jacobs, K. (2005). The sacred and the secular: examining the role of accounting in the religious context. *Accounting, Auditing & Accountability Journal*, *18*(2), 189–210. https://doi.org/10.1108/09513570510588724

Janvrin, D. J., Payne, E. A., Byrnes, P., Schneider, G. P., & Curtis, M. B. (2012). The updated COSO internal control--integrated framework: Recommendations and opportunities for future research. *Journal of Information Systems*, *26*(2), 189–213. https://doi.org/10.2308/isys-50255

Jensen, M. C. (1993). The modern industrial revolution, exit, and the failure of internal control systems. *Journal of Finance*, *48*(3), 831–880. https://doi.org/10.1111/j.1540-6261.1993.tb04022.x

Johnson, C. B., & Wright, C. J. (2004). Make it easy they will come: US corporations are liable for the criminal and fraudulent acts of their employees. But they can mitigate the risk by demonstrating a solid internal corporate compliance program for employee reporting. *Internal Auditor*, *61*(1), 69-75. https://go.gale.com/ps/anonymous?id=GALE%7CA113649525&sid=googleScholar&v=2.1&it=r&linkaccess=fulltext&issn=00205745&p=AONE&sw=w

Johnson, G. F., Hartong, R., & Kidd, B. (2014). Fraudtown, USA: Three essential internal controls for public sector entities. *The Journal of Government Financial Management*, *63*(4), 46–51. http://ezproxy.liberty.edu/login?url=https://search-proquest-com.ezproxy.liberty.edu/docview/1711619899?accountid=12085

Johnson, R., & Onwuegbuzie, A. (2004). Mixed methods research: A research paradigm whose time has come. *Educational Researcher*, *33*(7), 14–26. https://www.jstor.org/stable/3700093

Jonson, C. L., & Geis, G. (2010). Cressey, Donald R.: Embezzlement and white-collar crime. In F. T. Cullen & P. Wilcox (Eds.), *Encyclopedia of Criminological Theory* (Vol. 1, pp. 223–230). Sage.

Kaler, J. (2003). Differentiating stakeholder theories. *Journal of Business Ethics*, *46*(1), 71–83. https://doi.org/10.2307/25075089

Keats, P. A. (2009). Multiple text analysis in narrative research: visual, written, and spoken stories of experience. *Qualitative Research*, *9*(2), 181–195. https://doi.org/10.1177/1468794108099320

Kennedy, J. P. (2018). Asset misappropriation in small businesses. *Journal of Financial Crime*, *25*(2), 369–383. https://doi.org/10.1108/JFC-01-2017-0004

Kramer, B. (2015). Trust, but verify: Fraud in small businesses. *Journal of Small Business and Enterprise Development, 22*(1), 4–20. https://doi.org/10.1108/JSBED-08-2012-0097

Kranacher, M. J., Riley Jr, R. A., & Wells, J. T. (2011). *Forensic accounting and fraud examination.* Wiley.

Kummer, T., Singh, K., & Best, P. (2015). The effectiveness of fraud detection instruments in not-for-profit organizations. *Managerial Auditing Journal, 30*(4), 435–455. https://doi.org/10.1108/MAJ-08-2014-1083

Kunda, Z. (1990). The case for motivated reasoning. *Psychological Bulletin, 108*(3), 480–498. https://doi.org/10.1037/0033-2909.108.3.480

Lakis, V., & Giriunas, L. (2012). The concept of internal control system: Theoretical aspect. *Ekonomika, 91*(2), 142–152. https://doi.org/10.15388/Ekon.2012.0.890

Lee, S., Bolton, L. E., & Winterich, K. P. (2017). To profit or not to profit? The role of greed perceptions in consumer support for social ventures. *Journal of Consumer Research, 44*(4), 853–876. https://doi.org/10.1093/jcr/ucx071

Lee, S. A., Chancellor, R., Chu, C. M., Rodriguez-Mori, H., & Roy, L. (2015). Igniting diversity: Actionable methods and ideas for advancing diversity in LIS education in the US. *Journal of Education for Library and Information Science, 56,* S47–S60. https://doi.org/10.12783/issn.2328-2967/56/S1/6

Lenghel, R. D. (2015). Internal financial accounting control of private entities. *Quaestus*, (7), 120–131. https://www.quaestus.ro/en/wp-content/uploads/2012/02/lenghel.radu_.pdf

Lenz, A. S., Balkin, R. S., & Smith, R. L. (2017). *A counselor's guide to the dissertation process: Where to start and how to finish.* John Wiley & Sons.

Lowe, J. S., & Shipp, S. C. (2014). Black church and black college community development corporations: Enhancing the public sector discourse. *Western Journal of Black Studies*, *38*(4), 244–259. https://www.questia.com/library/journal/1G1-400785002/black-church-and-black-college-community-development

Lumpkin, A., & Achen, R. M. (2018). Explicating the synergies of self-determination theory, ethical leadership, servant leadership, and emotional intelligence. *Journal of Leadership Studies*, *12*(1), 6–20. https://doi.org/10.1002/jls.21554

Lunn, J. (2009). The role of religion, spirituality and faith in development: a critical theory approach. *Third World Quarterly*, *30*(5), 937–951. https://doi.org/10.1080/01436590902959180

Machado, M. R. R., & Gartner, I. R. (2018). The Cressey hypothesis (1953) and an investigation into the occurrence of corporate fraud: an empirical analysis conducted in Brazilian banking institutions. *Revista Contabilidade & Finanças - USP*, *29*(76), 60–81. https://doi.org/10.1590/1808-057x201803270

Mackevicius, J., & Giriunas, L. (2013). Transformational research of the Fraud Triangle. *Ekonomika*, *92*(4), 150–163. https://pdfs.semanticscholar.org/ea70/60d43086caff0a74284c2ac2f17c7a98c8c6.pdf

Majid, R. A., Basri, S. A., Mohamed, N., & Ahmad, K. (2016). The commitment of local authorities in building fortress against misappropriation of assets. *Malaysian Accounting Review*, *15*(2), 231–241. https://doi.org/10.24191/mar.v15i2.598

Mangala, D., & Kumari, P. (2017). Auditors' perceptions of the effectiveness of fraud prevention and detection methods. *Indian Journal of Corporate Governance*, *10*(2), 118–142. https://doi.org/10.1177/0974686217738683

Mayhew, B. W., & Murphy, P. R. (2014). The impact of authority on reporting behavior, rationalization and affect. *Contemporary Accounting Research*, *31*(2), 420-443. https://doi.org/10.1111/1911-3846.12037

Mazar, N., Amir, O., & Ariely, D. (2008). The dishonesty of honest people: A theory of self-concept maintenance. *Journal of Marketing Research*, *45*(6), 633–644. https://doi.org/10.1509/jmkr.45.6.633

McDonnell, D., & Rutherford, A. C. (2018). The determinants of charity misconduct. *Nonprofit & Voluntary Sector Quarterly*, *47*(1), 107–125. https://doi.org/10.1177/0899764017728367

McKeever, B. (2019). *National Center for Charitable Statistics. The Nonprofit Sector in Brief.* Retrieved from https://nccs.urban.org/project/nonprofit-sector-brief.

McMahon, R., Pence, D., Bressler, L., & Bressler, M. S. (2016). New tactics in fighting financial crimes: Moving beyond the fraud triangle. *Journal of Legal, Ethical and Regulatory Issues*, *19*(1), 16. https://www.researchgate.net/publication/312120199_New_tactics_in_fighting_financial_crimes_Moving_beyond_the_fraud_triangle

McNeal, A. (2016). What's your fraud IQ? This month: Employee handbooks and policies. *Journal of Accountancy*, *222*(3), 38–43. https://www.questia.com/library/journal/1G1-462141745/what-s-your-fraud-iq-this-month-employee-handbooks

Miceli, M. P., & Near, J. P. (1994). Whistleblowing: Reaping the benefits. *The Academy of Management Executive*, *8*(3), 65. https://doi.org/10.5465/AME.1994.9503101177

Milde, K., & Yawson, R. M. (2017). Strategies for social media use in nonprofits. *Journal of Management Policy and Practice*, *18*(1), 19–27. http://digitalcommons.www.na-businesspress.com/JMPP/MildeK_Web18_1_.pdf

Min, P. G., & Jang, S. H. (2015). The diversity of Asian immigrants' participation in religious institutions in the United States. *Sociology of Religion*, *76*(3), 253–274. https://doi.org/10.1093/socrel/srv025

Mock, T. J., Srivastava, R. P., & Wright, A. M. (2017). Fraud risk assessment using the fraud risk model as a decision aid. *Journal of Emerging Technologies in Accounting*, *14*(1), 37–56. https://doi.org/10.2308/jeta-51724

Moody, H. R., & Achenbaum, W. A. (2014). Solidarity, sustainability, stewardship: Ethics across generations. *Interpretation*, *68*(2), 150–158. https://doi.org/10.1177/0020964313517656

Moore, G. F., Audrey, S., Barker, M., Bond, L., Bonell, C., Hardeman, W., & Baird, J. (2015). Process evaluation of complex interventions: Medical research council guidance. *BMJ (Clinical Research Ed.)*, *350*. https://doi.org/10.1136/bmj.h1258

Morales, J., Gendron, Y., & Guenin-Paracini, H. (2014). The construction of the risky individual and vigilant organization: A genealogy of the fraud triangle. *Accounting, Organizations and Society*, *39*(3), 170–194. https://doi.org/10.1016/j.aos.2014.01.006

Morales, S. R., & Cabello, M. C. (2015). Integrating character in management: virtues, character strengths, and competencies. *Business Ethics: A European Review*, *24*, S156–S174. https://doi.org/10.1111/beer.12104

Muganga, L. (2015). The importance of hermeneutic theory in understanding and appreciating interpretive inquiry as a methodology. *Journal of Social Research & Policy*, *6*(1), 65–88. http://ezproxy.liberty.edu/login?url=https://search-proquest-com.ezproxy.liberty.edu /docview/1810270415?accountid=12085

Murphy, M. L. (2015). Preventing and detecting fraud at not-for-profits. *Journal of Accountancy, 220*(6), 77–83. https://www.journalofaccountancy.com/content/dam/jofa/issues/2015/dec/prevent-and-detect-fraud-dec-2015.pdf

Murphy, P. R. (2012). Attitude, Machiavellianism and the rationalization of misreporting. *Accounting, Organizations and Society*, *37*, 242–259. https://doi.org/10.1016/j.aos.2012.04.002

Murphy, P. R., & Free, C. (2016). Broadening the fraud triangle: instrumental climate and fraud. *Behavioral Research in Accounting*, *28*(1), 41–56. https://doi.org/10.2308/bria-51083

Myllymäki, E. R. (2014). The persistence in the association between section 404 material weaknesses and financial reporting quality. Auditing: *A Journal of Practice & Theory*, *33*(1), 93–116. https://doi.org/10.2308/ajpt-50570

Nakhid, C. (2015). Community advisory groups in research with "selective" communities: Pacific island youth in South Auckland, New Zealand. *International Journal of Interdisciplinary Social & Community Studies*, *10*(3), 37–49. https://doi.org/10.18848/2324-7576/cgp/v10i03/53543

Nasatir, S. B., & Friedman, P. B. (2014). Jewish "right start." *Journal of Jewish Communal Service*, *89*(1), 30–37. https://repository.library.northeastern.edu/files/neu:cj82q154q/fulltext.pdf

Nasir, N. A. B. M., Ali, M. J., & Ahmed, K. (2019). Corporate governance, board ethnicity and financial statement fraud: Evidence from Malaysia. *Accounting Research Journal*, 32(3), 514–531. https://doi.org/10.1108/ARJ-02-2018-0024

Nawawi, A., & Salin, A. S. A. P. (2018). Employee fraud and misconduct: Empirical evidence from a telecommunication company. *Information and Computer Security*, *26*(1), 129–144. https://doi.org/10.1108/ICS-07-2017-0046

Nezhina, T. G., & Brudney, J. L. (2012). Unintended? The effects of adoption of the Sarbanes-Oxley Act on nonprofit organizations. *Nonprofit Management & Leadership*, *22*(3), 321–346. https://doi.org/10.1002/nml.20057

Nindito, M. (2018). Financial statement fraud: perspective of the pentagon fraud model in Indonesia. *Academy of Accounting and Financial Studies Journal*, *22*(3), 1–9. https://www.abacademies.org/articles/Financial-Statement-Fraud-Perspective-of-the-Pentagon-Fraud-Model-in-Indonesia-1528-2635-22-2-199.pdf

Nishimuko, M. (2008). The role of faith-based organizations in building democratic process: Achieving universal primary education in Sierra Leone. *International Journal of Social Sciences*, *3*, 172–179. https://www.semanticscholar.org/paper/The-Role-of-Faith-based-Organizations-in-Building-Nishimuko/30ab9e6cc77888e49bdadeb3e5f07f5abc835637

Nwoye, T. N. (2018). *Internal controls and fraud in small businesses: A qualitative case study* (Publication No. 10743771) [Doctoral dissertation, Liberty University]. ProQuest Dissertations & Theses Global.

Nzinga, J., McGivern, G., & English, M. (2019). Hybrid clinical-managers in Kenyan hospitals. *Journal of Health Organization and Management*, 33(2), 173-187. https://doi.org/10.1108/JHOM-08-2017-0203

O'Gara, J. D. (2014). *Corporate fraud: Case studies in detection and prevention*. John Wiley & Sons, Inc.

Öksüz, B., & Ker-Dinçer, M. (2012). Putting heart and soul in education: Spiritually intelligent servant-leaders in educational institutions. *Gaziantep University Journal of Social Sciences*, *11*(4), 1009–1022. https://avesis.ege.edu.tr/yayin/84e6e710-bceb-4415-8b85-61fba9cf3fee/putting-heart-and-soul-in-education-spiritually-intelligent-servant-leaders-in-educational-institutions

Omidi, M., Min, Q., Moradinaftchali, V., & Piri, M. (2019). The efficacy of predictive methods in financial statement fraud. *Discrete Dynamics in Nature & Society*, 1–12. https://doi.org/10.1155/2019/4989140

Ortega-Rodríguez, C., Licerán-Gutiérrez, A., & Moreno-Albarracín, A. L. (2020). Transparency as a key element in accountability in non-profit organizations: A systematic literature review. *Sustainability*, *12*(14), 5834. https://doi.org/10.3390/su12145834

Palumbo, R. (2016). Challenging servant leadership in the nonprofit sector: The side effects of servant leadership. *The Journal of Nonprofit Education and Leadership*, *6*(2). https://doi.org/10.18666/JNEL-2016-V6-I2-6824

Palvo, W. (2013). "Walter." *Forbes*. Retrieved from http://www.forbes.com/sites/walterpavlo fraudthriving-in-U-S-churches-but-you-wouldnt-know-it/

Pamungkas, I. D., Ghozali, I., & Achmad, T. (2018). A pilot study of corporate governance and accounting fraud: The fraud diamond model. *Journal of Business and Retail Management Research*, *12*(2), 253-261. https://doi.org/10.24052/JBRMR/V12IS02APSOCGAAFTFDM

Patelli, L., & Pedrini, M. (2015). Is tone at the top associated with financial reporting aggressiveness? *Journal of Business Ethics*, *126*(1), 3–19. https://doi.org/10.1007/s10551-013-1994-6

Pedersen, B., Delmar, C., Falkmer, U., & Grønkjaer, M. (2016). Bridging the gap between interviewer and interviewee: developing an interview guide for individual interviews by means of a focus group. *Scandinavian Journal of Caring Sciences*, *30*(3), 631–638. https://doi.org/10.1111/scs.12280

Percy, W. H., & Kostere, K. (2015). Generic qualitative research in psychology. *The Qualitative Report*, *20*(2), 76–85. https://nsuworks.nova.edu. /tqr/vol20/iss2/7

Peters, C. S. (2015). *More than just good deeds: Fraud within religious organizations* (Publication No. 1599154) [Doctoral dissertation, Utica College]. ProQuest Dissertations & Theses Global.

Pezalla, A. E., Pettigrew, J., & Miller-Day, M. (2012). Researching the researcher-as-instrument: an exercise in interviewer self-reflexivity. *Qualitative Research*, *12*(2), 165–185. https://doi.org/10.1177/1468794111422107

Pickerd, J. S., Summers, S. L., & Wood, D. A. (2015). An examination of how entry-level staff auditors respond to tone at the top vis-à-vis tone at the bottom. *Behavioral Research in Accounting*, *27*(1), 79–98. https://doi.org/10.2308/bria-50918

Pierce, E. M., & Goldstein, J. (2018). ERM and strategic planning: A change in paradigm. *International Journal of Disclosure and Governance*, *15*(1), 51–59. https://doi.org/10.1057/s41310-018-0033-3

Polit, D. F., & Beck, C. T. (2012). *Nursing research: Generating and assessing evidence for nursing practice* (9th ed.). Wolters Kluwer.

Pouryousefi, S., & Frooman, J. (2019). The consumer scam: An agency-theoretic approach. *Journal of Business Ethics*, *154*(1), 1–12. https://doi.org/10.1007/s10551-017-3466-x

Prus, R. (2007). Human memory, social process, and the pragmatist metamorphosis: Ethnological foundations, ethnographic contributions, and conceptual challenges. *Journal of Contemporary Ethnography*, *36*(4), 378–437. https://doi.org/10.1177/0891241606299029

Pulido, R. (2018). What secular nonprofits can learn from religious donors. *Journal of Multidisciplinary Research (1947-2900)*, *10*(1-2), 129–136. https://theoxfordconclave.org/wp-content/uploads/2018/09/secular-nonprofits.pdf

Qadri, U. A., Hassan, S. S., & Sheikh, M. A. (2017). The mediating role of internal locus of control and job stress between spiritual intelligence and job performance. *Pakistan Journal of Commerce and Social Sciences*, *11*(2), 623–643. https://www.semanticscholar.org/paper/The-mediating-role-of-internal-locus-of-control-and-Qadri-Hassan/94f0f0c274f0362f5b1305d9e345cdbb76bf4727

Qusqas, F., & Kleiner, B. H. (2001). The difficulties of whistleblowers finding employment. *Management Research News*, *24*(3-4), 97–100. https://doi.org/10.1108/01409170110782702

Rae, K., Sands, J., & Subramaniam, N. (2017). Associations among the five components within COSO internal control- integrated framework as the underpinning of quality corporate governance. *Australasian Accounting Business & Finance Journal*, *11*(1), 28–54. https://doi.org/10.14453/aabfj.v11i1.4

Ramanath, R. (2016). Unpacking donor retention: Individual monetary giving to U.S.-based Christian faith-related, international nongovernmental organizations. *Religions*, *7*(11), 133. https://doi.org/10.3390/rel7110133

Rana, A., Anwar, A., & Hasan, M. N. (2017). Cognitive intelligence and spiritual management for effective managerial decision making. *Independent Business Review, 10*(1), 43–64. http://dir.iub.edu.bd:8080/xmlui/xmlui/handle/123456789/455

Recine, J. S. (2002). Examination of the white collar crime penalty enhancements in the Sarbanes-Oxley Act. *The American Criminal Law Review, 39*(4), 1535–1570. https://heinonline.org/HOL/LandingPage?handle=hein.journals/amcrimlr39&div=47&id=&page=

Ridder, H. (2017). The theory contribution of case study research designs. *Business Research, 10*(2), 281–305. https://doi.org/10.1007/s40685-017-0045-z

Roden, D. M., Cox, S. R., & Kim, J. Y. (2016). The fraud triangle as a predictor of corporate fraud. *Academy of Accounting and Financial Studies Journal, 20*(1), 80–92. https://www.researchgate.net/publication/304036915_The_Fraud_Triangle_as_a_Predictor_of_Corporate_Fraud

Rodgers, W., Söderbom, A., & Guiral, A. (2015). Corporate social responsibility enhanced control systems reducing the likelihood of fraud: *Journal of Business Ethics, 131*(4), 871–882. https://doi.org/10.1007/s10551-014-2152-5

Roland, D. R., & Harris, W. B. (2014). Information needs of church worship leaders. *Journal of Religious & Theological Information, 13*(1-2), 35–52. https://doi.org/10.1080/10477845.2014.921537.

Ross, S. A. (1973). The economic theory of agency: The principal's problem. *American Economic Review, 63*(2), 134–139. https://doi.org/10.2307/1817064

Russell, R. F., & Stone, A. G. (2002). A review of servant leadership attributes: Developing a practical model. *Leadership & Organization Development Journal*, *23*(3), 145–157. https://doi.org/10.1108/01437730210424

Rutberg, S., & Bouikidis, C. D. (2018). Focusing on the fundamentals: A simplistic differentiation between qualitative and quantitative research. *Nephrology Nursing Journal*, *45*(2), 209–212. http://www.homeworkgain.com/wp-content/uploads/edd/2019/09/20181009143525article2.pdf

Saat, N. F., Mohamed, I. S., Zakaria, N. B., & Omar, N. (2013). Factors determining level of internal controls implementation among nonprofit organizations in Malaysia. *Advances in Natural and Applied Sciences*, *7*(75), 425–434. http://link.galegroup.com.ezproxy.liberty .edu/apps/doc/A365687681/AONE?u =vic_liberty&sid=AONE&xid=6e3fc61e

Sabau, A. S. (2012). Survey of clustering based financial fraud detection research. *Informatica Economica*, *16*(1), 110–122. https://www.researchgate.net/publication/267686837 _Survey_of_Clustering_based_Financial_Fraud_Detection_Research

Said, J., Alam, M. M., Karim, Z. A., & Johari, R. J. (2018). Integrating religiosity into fraud triangle theory: findings on Malaysian police officers. *Journal of Criminological Research, Policy and Practice*, *4*(2), 111–123. https://doi.org/10.1108/JCRPP-09-2017-0027

Salin, A. S. A. P., Ab Manan, S. K., Kamaluddin, N., & Nawawi, A. (2017). The role of Islamic ethics to prevent corporate fraud. *International Journal of Business and Society*, *18*(S1), 113–128.

Sankaran, S., Dick, B., Shaw, K., Cartwright, C., Davies, A., Kelly, J., & Vindin, B. (2014). Application of scenario-based approaches in leadership research: An action research intervention as three sets of interlinked practices. *Systemic Practice & Action Research, 27*(6), 551-573. https://doi.org/10.1007/s11213-013-9308-6

Sanz, P., & Fontrodona, J. (2019). Moderation as a moral competence: Integrating perspectives for a better understanding of temperance in the workplace: JBE JBE. *Journal of Business Ethics, 155*(4), 981–994. https://doi.org/10.1007/s10551-018-3899-x.

Saxton, G. D., & Neely, D. G. (2019). The relationship between Sarbanes–Oxley policies and donor advisories in nonprofit organizations: JBE JBE. *Journal of Business Ethics, 158*(2), 333–351. https://doi.org/10.1007/s10551-018-3843-0

Schaubroeck, J. M., Hannah, S. T., Avolio, B. J., Kozlowski, S. W., Lord, R. G., Treviño, L. K., & Peng, A. C. (2012). Embedding ethical leadership within and across organization levels. *Academy of Management Journal, 55*(5), 1053–1078. https://doi.org/10.5465/amj.2011.0064

Schramm, W. (1971). *Notes on case studies of instructional media projects: Working papers for the academy for educational development*. Washington D.C.

Schuchter, A., & Levi, M. (2016). The fraud triangle revisited. *Security Journal, 29*(2), 107–121. https://doi.org/10.1057/sj.2013.1

Schürmann, E., & Beausaert, S. (2016). What are drivers for informal learning?. *European Journal of Training and Development, 40*(3), 130–153. https://doi.org/10.1108/EJTD-06-2015-0044

Segal, S. Y. (2016). Accounting frauds - review of advanced technologies to detect and prevent frauds. *Economics and Business Review*, *2*(4), 45–64. https://doi.org/10.18559/ebr.2016.4.3

Shaharuddin, S., & Sulaiman, M. (2015). Financial disclosure and budgetary practices of religious organization: A study of Qaryah Mosques in Kuala Terengganu. *Gadjah Mada International Journal of Business*, *17*(1), 83–101. https://doi.org/10.22146/gamaijb.6151

Shalvi, S., Gino, F., Barkan, R., & Ayal, S. (2015). Self-serving justifications: Doing wrong and feeling moral. *Current Directions in Psychological Science*, *24*(2), 125–130. https://doi.org/10.1177/0963721414553264

Sharma, A., & Panigrahi, P. K. (2013). A review of financial accounting fraud detection based on data mining techniques. *International Journal of Computer Applications* (0975-8887), *39*(1). https://doi.org/10.5120/4787-7016

Sherif, V. (2018). Evaluating preexisting qualitative research data for secondary analysis. *Forum: Qualitative Social Research*, *19*(2). https://doi.org/10.17169/FQS-19.2.2821

Shorten, A., & Moorley, C. (2014). Selecting the sample. *Evidence - Based Nursing*, *17*(2), 32. https://doi.org/10.1136/eb-2014-101747

Sider, R. J., & Unruh, H. R. (2004). Typology of religious characteristics of social service and educational organizations and programs. *Nonprofit and Voluntary Sector Quarterly*, *33*(1), 109–134. https://doi.org/10.1177/0899764003257494

Silverman, D. (2000). *Doing qualitative research: A practical guide*. Sage.

Simon, M. K., & Goes, J. (2013). *Dissertation and scholarly research: Recipes for success* (2013 Ed.). Dissertation Success, LLC.

Siswantoro, D., Rosdiana, H., & Fathurahman, H. (2018). Reconstructing accountability of the cash waqf (endowment) institution in Indonesia. *Managerial Finance*, *44*(5), 624-644. https://doi.org/10.1108/MF-05-2017-0188

Smaili, N., & Arroyo, P. (2019). Categorization of whistleblowers using the whistleblowing triangle. *Journal of Business Ethics*, *157*(1), 95–117. https://doi.org/10.1007/s10551-017-3663-7

Smith, K., Thew, G., & Graham, B. (2018). Conducting ethical internet-based research with vulnerable populations: a qualitative study of bereaved participants' experiences of online questionnaires. *European Journal of Psychotraumatology*, *9*(sup1), 1506231. https://doi.org/10.1080/20008198.2018.1506231

Sokolowski, R. (2000). *Introduction to phenomenology.* Cambridge University Press.

Solomon, R. C. (2003). *A better way to think about business: How personal integrity leads to corporate success*. Oxford University Press.

Soltani, B. (2014). The anatomy of corporate fraud: A comparative analysis of high profile American and European corporate scandals. *Journal of Business Ethics*, *120*(2), 251–274. https://doi.org/10.1007/s10551-013-1660-z

Sorunke, O. A. (2016). Personal ethics and fraudster motivation: The missing link in fraud triangle and fraud diamond theories. *International Journal of Academic Research in Business and Social Sciences*, *6*(2), 159–165. https://doi.org/10.6007/IJARBSS/v6-i2/2020

Spears, L. C. (2010). Character and servant leadership: Ten characteristics of effective, caring leaders. *The Journal of Virtues & Leadership*, *1*(1), 25–30. https://www.regent.edu/acad/global/publications/jvl/vol1_iss1/Spears_Final.pdf

Srivastava, A., & Thomson, S. B. (2009). *Framework analysis: A qualitative methodology for applied policy research*. https://papers.ssrn.com/sol3/papers.cfm?abstract_id=2760705

Stake, R. E. (2010). *Qualitative research: Studying how things work.* Guilford Press.

Starks, H., & Trinidad, S. B. (2007). Choose your method: a comparison of phenomenology, discourse analysis, and grounded theory. *Qualitative Health Research*, *17*(10), 1372–1380. https://doi.org/10.1177/1049732307307031

Steimel, S. (2018). Skills-based volunteering as both work and not work: A tension-centered examination of constructions of “volunteer”. *VOLUNTAS: International Journal of Voluntary and Nonprofit Organizations*, *29*(1), 133–143. https://doi.org/10.1007/s11266-017-9859-8

Stephens, J., & Flaherty, M. P. (2013). Inside the hidden world of thefts, scams and phantom purchases at the nation’s nonprofits. *The Washington Post.* http://www.washingtonpost.com.

Suárez, C. A. (2017). Internal control systems leading to family business performance in Mexico: A framework analysis. *Journal of International Business Research*, *16*(1), 1–16. https://www.abacademies.org/articles/internal-control-systems-leading-to-family-business-performance-in-mexico-a-framework-analysis-6881.html

Sulaiman, M., Siraf, S. A., & Mohamed Ibrahim, S. H. (2008). Internal control systems in West Malaysia’s state mosques. *American Journal of Islamic Social Sciences*, *25*(1), 63–81. https://doi.org/10.35632/AJISS.V25I1.396

Tak, I. (2015). Proactive approach for the impacts of fraudulent financial information on economic decision. *Scientific Papers: Management, Economic Engineering in Agriculture & Rural Development*, *15*(4), 335–343. http://managementjournal.usamv.ro/pdf/vol.15_4/vol15_4.pdf

Thompson, C. J. (1997). Interpreting consumers: A hermeneutical framework for deriving marketing insights from the texts of consumers' consumption stories. *Journal of Marketing Research (JMR)*, *34*(4), 438–455. https://doi.org/10.1177/002224379703400403

Thomson, D. R., Semakula, M., Hirschhorn, L. R., Murray, M., Ndahindwa, V., Manzi, A., Mukabutera, A., Karema, C., Condo, J., & Hedt-Gauthier, B. (2016). Applied statistical training to strengthen analysis and health research capacity in Rwanda. *Health Research Policy and Systems*, *14*(1), 73. https://doi.org/10.1186/s12961-016-0144-x

Thornhill, R., & Domino, M. A. (2016). Passing the plate: A survey of internal controls in local churches. *Journal of Theoretical Accounting Research*, *12*(1), 26–53. https://works.bepress.com/carmelita_troy/2/

Tinkelman, D. P., & Song, Y. (2012). If asset misappropriation is so common, why do so few public companies disclose it? *Journal of Forensic Studies in Accounting & Business*, *4*(1), 65–82. https://www.researchgate.net/publication/323830248_If_Asset_Misappropriation_Is_So_Common_Why_Do_So_Few_Public_Companies_Disclose_It

Tiwari, R. K., & Debnath, J. (2017). Forensic accounting: a blend of knowledge. *Journal of Financial Regulation and Compliance*, *25*(1), 73–85. https://doi.org/10.1108/JFRC-05-2016-0043

Toner, P., & Woolley, R. (2016). Perspectives and debates on vocational education and training, skills and the prospects for innovation. *Revista Espanola De Sociologia*, *25*(3), 319–342. https://doi.org/10.22325/fes/res.25.3.2016.319

Tschakert, N., Needles Jr, B., & Holtzblatt, M. (2016). The red flags of fraud: Internal auditors' knowledge of the business makes them ideal candidates to detect unethical behaviors. *Internal Auditor*, *73*(5), 60. https://go.gale.com/ps/anonymous?id=GALE%7CA467829998&sid=googleScholar&v=2.1&it=r&linkaccess=abs&issn=00205745&p=AONE&sw=w

Tushe, I. (2016). The New York Nonprofit Revitalization Act, from the foundation of the Sarbanes-Oxley Act to implementation. *International Journal of Not-for-Profit Law*, *18*(1), 65–77. https://www.icnl.org/resources/research/ijnl/volume-18-issue-1

Vandekerckhove, W. (2018). Whistleblowing and information ethics: Facilitation, entropy, and ecopoiesis: JBE JBE. *Journal of Business Ethics*, *152*(1), 15–25. https://doi.org/10.1007/s10551-016-3294-4

Van Dierendonck, D. (2011). Servant leadership: A review and synthesis. *Journal of Management*, *37*, 1228–1261. https://doi.org/10.1177/0149206310380462

Van Duzer, J. (2010). *Why business matters to God: (And what still needs to be fixed)*. IVP Academic.

Van Gelder, G. C., & Zscheile, D. (2018). *Participating in God's mission: A theological missiology for the church in America*. Wm. B. Eerdmans.

Varchuk, O. A., & Grabovenko, O. A. (2016). Internal control and internal audit: definition, similarities and differences. *Economics: Time Realities*, (1), 123–131. http://search.ebscohost.com.ezproxy.liberty.edu/login.aspx?direct=true&db=asn&AN=115555922&site=ehost-live&scope=site

Vasileiou, K., Barnett, J., Thorpe, S., & Young, T. (2018). Characterising and justifying sample size sufficiency in interview-based studies: Systematic analysis of qualitative health research over a 15-year period. *BMC Medical Research Methodology*, *18*, 148. https://doi.org/10.1186/s12874-018-0594-7

Ventura, M., & Daniel, S. J. (2010). Opportunities for fraud and embezzlement in religious organizations: An exploratory study. *Journal of Forensic and Investigative Accounting*, *2*(1), 1–35. http://web.nacva.com/JFIA/Issues/JFIA-2010-1_8.pdf

Warren, D. E., Peytcheva, M., & Gaspar, J. P. (2015). When ethical tones at the top conflict: adapting priority rules to reconcile conflicting Tones. *Business Ethics Quarterly*, *25*(4), 559–582. https://doi.org/10.1017/BEQ.2015.40

Wasylyshyn, K. M., & Gronsky, B. (2004). Emotional competence: Preliminary results of a coaching program commissioned by Rohm and Haas Company. *People and Strategy*, *27*(4), 7. https://go.gale.com/ps/anonymous?id=GALE%7CA126653493&sid=googleScholar&v=2.1&it=r&linkaccess=abs&issn=01998986&p=AONE&sw=w

Webster. (2019). *Webster's online dictionary*. https://www.merriam-webster.com/dictionary/fraud?utm_campaign=sd&utm_medium=serp&utm_source=jsonld

Wells, J. T. (2013). *Corporate fraud handbook: Prevention and detection*. https://ebookcentral-proquest-com.ezproxy.liberty.edu

Wilbanks, D. (2016). The Sarbanes-Oxley Act: Relevant to OSH Practice?. *Professional Safety, 61*(2), 23–25. https://search.proquest.com/docview/1765137307?pq-origsite=gscholar&fromopenview=true

Winterich, K. P., & Zhang, Y. (2014). Accepting inequality deters responsibility: how power distance decreases charitable behavior. *Journal of Consumer Research, 41*(2), 274–293. https://doi.org/10.1086/675927

Wolfe, D. T., & Hermanson, D. R. (2004). The fraud diamond: Considering the four elements of fraud. *The CPA Journal*, *74*(12), 38–42. https://pdfs.semanticscholar.org/c9c8/32fa299f648464cbd0172ff293f5c35684b6.pdf

Wooten, T. C., Coker, J. W., & Elmore, R. C. (2003). Financial control in religious organizations: A status report. *Nonprofit Management and Leadership*, *13*(4), 343–365. https://doi.org/10.1002/nml.4

Xu, B., Bhuiyan, M. B. U., & Rahman, A. (2016). Underlying profit in New Zealand. *Pacific Accounting Review*, *28*(2), 111–134. https://doi.org/10.1108/PAR-01-2016-0006

Yallapragada, R. R., Roe, C. W., & Toma, A. G. (2012). Accounting fraud, and white-collar crimes in the United States. *Journal of Business Case Studies (Online)*, *8*(2), 187. https://doi.org/10.19030/jbcs.v8i2.6806

Yasin, F., Muhamad, R., & Sulaiman, N. A. (2014). Corporate governance research: A review of qualitative literature. *Paper presented at the International Conference on Technology and Business Management*, Dubai, UAE.

Yasmin, S., Haniffa, R., & Hudaib, M. (2014). Communicated accountability by faith-based charity organizations. *Journal of Business Ethics*, *122*(1), 103–123. https://doi.org/10.1007/s10551-013-1759-2

Yin, R. K. (2014). *Case study research: Design and methods* (5th ed.). Sage.

Zain, N. R. B. M., Hassan, R., & Mustaffha, N. (2018). Waqf institutions in Malaysia: Appreciation of Wasaṭiyyah approach in internal control as a part of good governance. *Intellectual Discourse*, *26*(2), 749–764. http://ezproxy.liberty.edu/login?url =https://search-proquest-com.ezproxy.liberty.edu/docview/2164442289?accountid =12085

Zask, E. (2014). Finding financial fraudsters: Quantitative and behavioral finance approaches. *Journal of Securities Operations & Custody*, *6*(4), 308–324. http://search.ebscohost.com.ezproxy.liberty.edu/login.aspx?direct=true&db=bth&AN=97 359270&site=ehost-live&scope=site

Zohar, D. (2005). Spiritually intelligent leadership. *Leader to Leader*, *2005*(38), 45–51. https://doi.org/10.1002/ltl.153

Zulkipli, N. H., & Baba, S. (2018). Challenges and strengths in conducting a qualitative analysis. *Malaysian Journal of Qualitative Research*, *4*(1), 53–59.

Zurlo, G. (2015). The social gospel, ecumenical movement, and Christian sociology: the institute of social and religious research. *American Sociologist*, *46*(2), 177–193. https://doi.org/10.1007/s12108-014-9231-z.

Appendix A:

Interview Questions

1. What competencies, accounting education, and accounting experience do you possess as your organization's financial administrator that enable you to understand financial internal controls?

2. What is your full time professional or job inside and/or outside of your organization?

3. Gender:
   a) M
   b) F

4. Age
   a. 20 – 29
   b. 30- 39
   c. 40 – 49
   d. 50 – 59
   e. 60+

5. General Education Level
   a) High School Diploma/GED
   b) Some college or technical training
   c) Bachelor's degree
   d) Master or Higher

6. Specialized Accounting or Financial certification
   a. General Education Level
   b. Certified Public Accountant (CPA)
   c. Certified Financial Planner(CFA)
   d. Certified Management accountant(CMA)
   e. Other

7. What is the nature of services that your religious organization provides to the public?

8. What is the size of your religious entity's budget?

9. What is your leadership role in the entity?

10. Are you employed as a paid employee or as a paid or unpaid volunteer?

11. In your role, do you provide financial management support in the organization?

12. How long have you served in your role in making financial decisions for the religious enterprise?

13. What financial training have you taken to support your leadership role in your religious organization?

14. Who do you believe has the fiduciary responsibility and oversight for protecting the organization's resources?

15. How has your professional or non-professional experience equipped you to detect potential fraud, mismanagement, misappropriation, or abuse in your religious entity?

16. What types of decisions have you made concerning the financial management of the church's resources?

17. What measures, if any, does your organization have in place to deal with massive fraud or misappropriation of funds?

18. What type of fund raising efforts your organization is involved with?

19. Does the fund raising efforts include high cash transactions?

20. Do you feel that your religious enterprise is fully protected against fraud?

21. What control activities are in place by management to dissuade fraud theft and fraudulent activities?

22. What additional training is required for you to strengthen your financial competencies to safeguard the organization's resources adequately?

23. What is your opinion of implementing the following practices to enhance financial stewardship of the organization's leaders?
    a) Creating segregation of duties for the accounting operations if not already in place
    b) Having a CPA or a qualified financial professional annually audit the organization financial statements
    c) Creating checks and balances of bookkeeping procedures

24. Describe your understanding of sound financial accounting principles such as generally accepted accounting principles or the accounting regulations issued by the Financial Accounting Standard Board as it relates to the religious organizations?

25. What internal control does your organization have in place to deal with fraud committed by leadership versus fraud committed by non-leadership?

26. How do you feel about the financial transparency of the organization?

27. Describe if your organization has ever done a risk assessment to determine its vulnerability to fraud?

28. Are you and your Board of directors satisfied with the organization's ability to detect and deter fraud?

29. Describe how you, as an enterprise leader would respond to acts of fraud, waste, mismanagement, abuse, or misappropriation in the church?

30. When you hear about fraudulent actions against the religious organization, how do you feel, and do these stories cause you to look at your current internal control?

31. What else do you want to share regarding your ability to promote sound financial stewardship in securing the entity's resources?

32. What ongoing training, if any, does your organization have in place for its leaders and financial stewards?

33. Are there any questions or comments you would like to add?

Made in United States
North Haven, CT
05 November 2026

21768313R00109